THE PRACTICE OF CORPORATE GOVERNANCE

All corporate entities, from the largest multinational conglomerate to the smallest tennis club, need effective governance. Some features of corporate governance are basic, common to all corporate entities: every governing body needs to think strategically and set policies to supervise ongoing management activities to ensure the entity is financially viable and is achieving its objectives.

Every corporate entity has a governing body, whether it is called a board of directors, a committee, a council, or anything else. Many people, when appointed to the governing body of an organisation, have little idea of what to expect and what is expected of them. Even those with board-level experience find that the culture and leadership style of other governing bodies differ. The aim of this book is to help them understand and improve their contribution to the organisation and governing body they serve. The book is a simple guide to the work of every board member.

Each chapter concludes with a worksheet, which enables readers to apply the ideas in that chapter to their own organisation. On completing the book, readers will have a detailed analysis of the governance of their own organisation.

Effective governance improves performance and ensures long-term success. This book offers a straightforward guide to the fundamental work of governing bodies and the people who serve on them.

Bob Tricker left school at 16, qualified as a Chartered Accountant, served as an officer in the Royal Navy, was Financial Controller of the British subsidiary of an American steel company, and then studied at Harvard and Oxford Universities. His research as a Research Fellow of Nuffield College, Oxford, produced the book *Corporate Governance* (1984), the first with that title. He has held professorial appointments at universities in Hong Kong, Melbourne, New York, Oxford, Sydney, and Warwick. He now lives in Devon, continues to write, and has been the Deputy Launch Authority for the Torbay lifeboat and crewed on Brixham's heritage sailing trawlers.

THE PRACTICE OF CORPORATE GOVERNANCE

Bob Tricker

CRC Press
Taylor & Francis Group
Boca Raton London New York

CRC Press is an imprint of the
Taylor & Francis Group, an **informa** business

First Edition published 2023

by CRC Press
6000 Broken Sound Parkway NW, Suite 300, Boca Raton, FL 33487-2742

and by CRC Press
4 Park Square, Milton Park, Abingdon, Oxon, OX14 4RN

CRC Press is an imprint of Taylor & Francis Group, LLC

© 2023 Bob Tricker

Library of Congress Cataloging-in-Publication Data
Names: Tricker, R. Ian (Robert Ian) author.
Title: The practice of corporate governance / Bob Tricker.
Description: 1 Edition. | Boca Raton : CRC Press, 2023. | Includes
bibliographical references and index.
Identifiers: LCCN 2022020483 (print) | LCCN 2022020484 (ebook) | ISBN
9781032342399 (hardback) | ISBN 9781032342405 (paperback) | ISBN
9781003321132 (ebook)
Subjects: LCSH: Corporate governance.
Classification: LCC HD2741 .T713 2023 (print) | LCC HD2741 (ebook) | DDC
658.4--dc23/eng/20220427
LC record available at https://lccn.loc.gov/2022020483
LC ebook record available at https://lccn.loc.gov/2022020484

ISBN: 978-1-032-34239-9 (hbk)
ISBN: 978-1-032-34240-5 (pbk)
ISBN: 978-1-003-32113-2 (ebk)

DOI: 10.1201/9781003321132

Typeset in Caslon
by SPi Technologies India Pvt Ltd (Straive)

Dedicated, with gratitude, to the countless board members, chairs, corporate governance professionals, academic colleagues, and students around the world who, over the years, have contributed advice, experience, and insights that have led to my appreciation and understanding of the fascinating subject of corporate governance. I owe them a lot.

Contents

X   CONTENTS

Acknowledgements

The book benefited significantly from the editorial efforts of my daughter, Nicky, and Ray Bedder, friend, neighbour, and himself a company director and chair, who assiduously commented on each chapter as it appeared. I am also grateful for editorial guidance from my publisher, Gabriella Williams and her colleagues. The book could not have been written without the dictation software and magnification equipment provided by Blind Veterans UK (I was in the Royal Navy for a while).

Prologue
What This Book Is About

During the second half of the 20th century, organisations were fascinated by management: management theories, management consultants, and management gurus proliferated. However, in the early decades of the 21st century, interest has swung from the management of organisations to their governance.

Many people, when they are appointed to the governing body of an organisation, have little idea of what to expect and what is expected of them. Even those with board-level experience find that the culture and leadership style of other governing bodies differ. The aim of this book is to help them understand and improve their contribution to the organisation and governing body they serve. The book is not a legal treatise for the lawyer or company secretary, nor is it a textbook for an MBA course in corporate governance. It is a simple guide to the work of the board member.

All corporate entities, from the largest multi-national conglomerate to the smallest tennis club need effective governance. Every corporate entity has a governing body, whether it is called a board of directors, a committee, a council, or anything else. Some features of corporate governance are basic, common to all corporate entities, whatever their size, structure, or purpose, wherever they are located, and whoever form their membership. For example, every entity needs to think strategically, to supervise ongoing management activities, to ensure the entity is financially viable, and is achieving its objectives.

Effective governance improves performance and ensures long-term success. This book offers a straightforward guide to the fundamental work of governing bodies and the people who serve on them.

How to Benefit from This Book

The basic premise of this book is that all corporate entities need to be governed, whatever their purpose, structure, or size; better they are governed well. Every member of a governing body, whether called a director, counsellor, committee member, or any other name, will find the book useful. Readers will find the book most useful if they relate it to their own governance situation.

Each chapter ends with a worksheet, which enables readers to confirm they have understood the material and to relate it to their own organisation. On conclusion, these worksheets form a valuable workbook that describes and analyses the governance of the reader's own organisation.

This workbook can be used in various ways:

1. As a personal summary of the reader's own understanding of corporate governance
2. As the basis of a personal report that could be passed to the Chair for consideration
3. As the basis for a board-level assessment project, in which the Chair, with the approval of all board members, uses the workbook for each director to critique that organisation's governance and identify opportunities for change.

The worksheets could also be used as the basis for a board-level review conducted with the Chair and board approval, by one of the non-executive directors or an independent expert.

If the completed workbook is turned into a report, it is important to have the approval of the Chair and all other members of the governing body whose contribution will be covered. Inevitably, the report will contain judgements on the characteristics and quality of board leadership and the contribution of individual board members. Because it contains personal data, a report must meet the relevant Privacy Law and avoid possible libel or defamation actions.

For some organisations, the report will contain information that could be valuable outside the organisation. For example, in a listed, public company the report could contain share price-sensitive information. It may contain data of value to competitors. It might also have a reputational effect if leaked to the media or the market.

Given the potential sensitivity of the report, establishing its security level is vital and it should meet the organisation's security protocols, including the distribution-list, access restrictions, method of transfer (including encryption of electronic transmission), storage requirements, and final disposal.

So that readers can complete the workbook online, a pro forma of a blank workbook is available on the author's website www.BobTricker.co.uk. This pro forma has been written in Microsoft Word so that material can be included and spaced as appropriate. The eight-chapter headings can provide sections for the report and the questions can readily be turned into subheadings.

The Background to This Book

The book is rooted in research, including five years' work by the author as a Research Fellow of Nuffield College, Oxford, which led to the first book with the title *Corporate Governance*.[1] As founder – editor of the research journal, *Corporate Governance – an international review*,[2] the author has been able to follow subsequent developments in practice, law, and research. Teaching corporate governance courses in business schools around the world, has honed that knowledge. His corporate governance textbook,[3] which is widely used in business school MBA courses, is too detailed for most practising directors: this book attempts to highlight the basics.

In the author's experience, having served on the boards of profit-orientated companies, not-for-profit organisations, including a hospital trust, voluntary organisations, and a charity, as well as government committees, there is a need for this book. Consulting projects and strategy seminars, run for boards of directors around the world, have reinforced that conviction.

It is sincerely hoped that this book will enable readers to improve their contribution to the governance of the organisations they serve and demonstrate that corporate governance is a fascinating subject.

Notes

1 Tricker, R. I. (1984), *Corporate Governance*, Gower Press, London and The Corporate Policy Group, Oxford.
2 https://onlinelibrary.wiley.com/journal/14678683
3 Tricker, Bob, *Corporate Governance – principles, policies, and practices* (4th edition 2019), Oxford University Press.

1

ALL CORPORATE ENTITIES NEED CORPORATE GOVERNANCE

Modern society operates through corporate entities – companies, clubs, cooperatives, institutions, societies, joint ventures, partnerships, societies, trusts, and unions. Although their formats, purposes, and scale vary significantly, they all have one thing in common: they all need to be managed, and they all need to be governed. In this book, we shall focus on the governance of corporate entities, a process, unsurprisingly, known as corporate governance. However, it is perhaps surprising that the basic elements of corporate governance apply to every corporate entity.

All corporate entities are created to meet a need and fulfil a purpose to satisfy its members. For example, a company is incorporated to generate value for its shareholders and other stakeholders, a club is opened to provide recreational facilities for its members, or a professional body is formed to set entry standards and regulate its members.

The Constitution

Underpinning every corporate entity is its constitution. For a limited-liability company, this is its memorandum and articles of association; the constitution for a partnership is the partnership agreement, for a chartered professional institution its constitution is its formal charter, while for a club, its constitution may be no more than a set of rules.

Nevertheless, every corporate entity needs a constitution. Without a written constitution a group of people acting together is not really a

DOI: 10.1201/9781003321132-1

1

corporate entity. The constitution defines a corporate entity, identifying its name, its members, and its purpose. A constitution is likely to contain at least:

- the name of the corporate entity
- its objectives or purpose
- its members, their rights, and their duties
- its governing body and how its members are nominated and elected
- its finances, keeping accounts, audit, and reporting to members

The articles of association of even a small limited-liability company may contain hundreds of detailed clauses, identifying the rules by which the company is governed. In essence, the constitution defines the corporate entity and the way it is governed.

The Legal Context

A corporate entity is constrained by the laws of the jurisdiction in which it is incorporated and operates. In the case of limited-liability companies, this is the company law and corporate regulation, for partnerships the relevant partnership law, and for other entities including charities, cooperatives, and trade unions, laws enacted for these sectors. In a few cases, where the state has a particular interest in an enterprise, a corporate entity may operate under its own law. Those involved in the governance of corporate entities are not expected to be experts in the relevant law but do need to be aware of its context so that they can seek appropriate advice.

Defining Corporate Governance

Some definitions of corporate governance focus on 'the way companies are directed and controlled.' This tends to put the emphasis on conformance and compliance. Here, we take a broader view, suggesting that corporate governance is the way power is exercised over a corporate entity and is held accountable. This definition enables us to focus on the governing body's responsibility for corporate performance as well as corporate compliance.

The Members

Fundamentally, all corporate entities are created to serve the needs of their members. In the case of companies, members are the shareholders who own the company. In the case of partnerships, it is the partners. In many other organisations, membership is apparent because members are registered and pay subscriptions. The rights and duties of such members are enshrined in that entity's constitution.

However, there are corporate entities in which the membership is less clear, often because a self-perpetuating set of directors dominates the enterprise. The actual members of such entities may only be established by the parties who would be entitled, under the law, to share the proceeds if the enterprise was wound up. But in most cases, the members of a corporate entity are apparent, and their rights, privileges, and duties are enshrined in that entity's constitution.

The members of a corporate entity provide the root of corporate governance power. In a limited-liability company, for example, the shareholder members have the right to nominate and appoint the directors, approve the directors' report and financial accounts presented to them, appoint the independent external auditors, and agree to dividends and changes in share capital. That is the legal position: in practice, the reality can be strikingly different, with companies dominated by self-appointed and self-perpetuating directorate elites, a situation we will be exploring later.

We should also note that some corporate entities, including many charities, create a form of corporate membership for contributors, who may not have power under that entity's constitution. Essentially, a fund-raising mechanism, such members may be given certain privileges, but they have no governance power under the constitution.

The Governing Body

Every corporate entity must be governed, so all need a governing body. Although, governing bodies are given many different names: the board of directors, the council, the committee, the court, or indeed, as in some Oxford colleges, just 'the governing body.' Similarly, the members of the governing body can have different titles: a director, a partner, a council member, a committee member, a trustee, or indeed a 'member of the governing body.'

To avoid repetition, from now on throughout this book, we will refer to the corporate entity as 'the company' or 'the corporate entity,' its governing body as 'the board,' and the members of the governing body as 'directors.' Readers will readily substitute the naming they use for their own governing body and its members. The worksheet, at the end of each chapter, will reinforce this substitution.

Governance and Management

Management is the decision-making and leadership process, using resources such as finance, people, and other assets, to achieve results. Corporate governance is the process that oversees management, ensuring that the entity is being well managed and is running in the right direction. Some definitions in Wikipedia confuse the two. In other words, management runs the enterprise: corporate governance assures that it is being well managed and is running in the right direction.

Management structures can usually be depicted as a hierarchy of relationships: each member of management knows to whom they report and who reports to them, up to the ultimate boss. The classical organisation chart (Figure 1.1) depicts the management hierarchy but does not include the board.

The chief executive delegates responsibility down the organisation structure, with the appropriate authority, and expects accountability

Figure 1.1   The classical triangle of management.

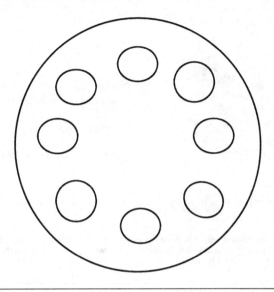

Figure 1.2 The circle of the board.

and performance in response. The board of directors seldom appears on the classical management organisation chart. Why not?

The board is not a hierarchy, nor is it part of management. Each director has the same power and is equally responsible for the work of the board. In addition, the board chair has a vital leadership role, as we will discuss later.

Consequently, the board is better depicted as a circle, showing directors with equal power and responsibility, not a hierarchy (Figure 1.2).

Executive and Non-Executive Directors

But, although all directors have equal responsibilities as members of the board, an important distinction needs to be made between executive directors and non-executive directors. As the name implies, executive directors hold executive positions in management in addition to their role as directors. Non-executive directors, sometimes called *outside directors*, are not part of the management team. In Figure 1.3 the circle of the board has been superimposed on the triangle of management, enabling us to clearly distinguish the executive and non-executive directors.

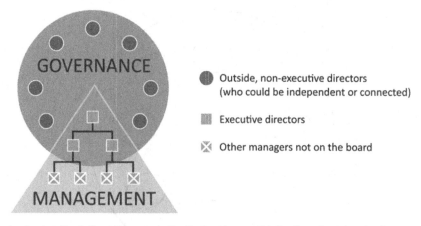

A unitary board has both outside, non-executive directors (shown as ● in the diagram) and executive directors (shown as a ▮ in the diagram). Executive directors have to 'wear two hats' – as directors on the board and as top executives in the management hierarchy.

Figure 1.3   The board and management.

In Figure 1.3, the board has ten directors, seven non-executive directors (shown as circles), and three executive directors (shown as squares), being members of both the board and the management team.

It is immediately obvious that there are alternative board structures:

- the board comprised entirely of non-executive directors
- the board with a majority of non-executive directors
- the board with a majority of executive directors
- the board comprised entirely of executive directors

Each of these boards has a legitimate place in corporate governance, which we will discuss in Chapter 2.

The Workbook

Each chapter concludes with a worksheet, which is a self-assessment report on aspects of corporate governance covered in that chapter. So readers can assess their own corporate governance situation and their contribution to it.

By the end of this book, the eight reports combined will provide a comprehensive report on the corporate governance in the reader's own situation. It may also highlight opportunities for improving their own and the overall board performance.

Corporate Governance Workbook

Worksheet #1

1. The name of the corporate entity
2. When was it founded or incorporated?
3. What is its constitution?

For example:

- the memorandum of incorporation and articles of association of a limited-liability company
- the rules of a co-operative society or a trade union
- the charter of a chartered professional body
- the partnership agreement in a partnership

4. What is the legal basis of your corporate entity?

For example:

- a company incorporated under company law
- a partnership operating under partnership law
- a registered society operating under the laws of, for example, co-operative societies, building societies (savings and loan associations), or credit unions
- a trust operating under the trust law
- a charitable society operating under the regulations governing charities
- a private organisation operating under the law of the relevant jurisdiction

5. Obtain a copy of the constitution.

Are you conversant with its provision on the following:

- purpose, objectives
- members, and their rights and duties
- registered office
- structure of the board
- nomination and appointment of members of the governing body
- preparation and presentation of accounts
- audit
- winding up

6. Who are the members of your corporate entity? Provide some statistics: Are there categories with different privileges or voting rights, how many?
7. What part do the members play in the governance of the entity?
8. Sketch the structure of your governing body on the following 'board circle and management triangle' diagram – show executive directors in both the circle and triangle as squares and non-executive directors outside the management as circles (at this stage, do not attempt to analyse the calibre of the board; we will do that in Chapter 2) (Figure 1.4)

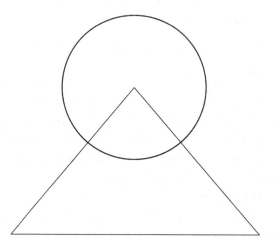

Figure 1.4   The structure of the reader's own board.

9. Consider the size of the board. Is the overall size of the board reasonable (too many, too few)? How might this be developed in the future?
10. Is the balance between executive and non-executive directors appropriate?

2

BOARD STRUCTURE AND BOARD MEMBERS

Directors: Executive and Non-Executive

Executive Directors

Executive directors are both members of the board and of management. They are in both the governance circle and the management triangle, in our diagram. Inevitably, therefore, they must wear two hats: as part of management they are responsible for running the enterprise, as directors they are responsible for governing the enterprise, including overseeing its management. This apparent dilemma can be overcome by adding independent non-executive directors to the board.

Independent Non-Executive, Outside Directors

An independent non-executive director, often called an outside director, has no connections with the enterprise which could influence the exercise of genuinely independent judgement. The corporate governance codes that apply to companies listed on stock exchanges around the world clarify such independence in some detail. For example, to be genuinely independent, a director should:

- not have a significant financial interest in the company
- not be a representative of a major shareholder
- not be related to anyone on the board or in the senior management
- not have recently served as an executive in that company
- not be a representative of those with financial or trading links to the company.

DOI: 10.1201/9781003321132-2

Some corporate governance codes limit the time a non-executive director may serve, arguing that long service might imply too close a connection with management.

Connected Non-Executive, Outside Directors

Of course, there may be people with some of these characteristics, whom the directors want to have on the board. Indeed, the criteria for granting a loan or entering into an agreement with the company might include the requirement to have a representative on the board. However, in these cases, the director though non-executive would not be recognised as independent. Such people are sometimes called connected non-executive directors.

Five Alternative Board Structures

The All-Executive Board

In many start-up enterprises, the board consists of the founder(s) and key executives. All the directors are also management executives. They may have difficulty in distinguishing their roles as managers from their responsibilities as directors, because day-to-day management issues crowd out longer term strategic thought and policy-making (Figure 2.1).

If the enterprise flourishes the distinction will become important. As we will see later, the board has specific responsibilities for formulating strategy and setting policy that transcends management duties.

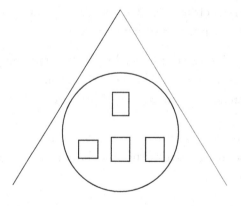

Figure 2.1   The all-executive board.

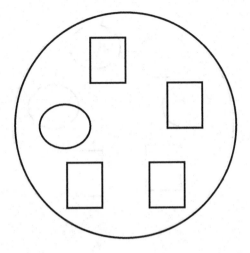

Figure 2.2   The majority executive board.

The Majority Executive Board

As the enterprise grows, the directors may feel the need for additional support on the board. This may be because they want additional managerial support. Perhaps, the entity is not yet able to afford a full-time executive with certain specialisms, but needs advice on finance, marketing, or human resource management. Or there may be someone who has experience, information, or network contacts relevant to the company. Ultimately, the founder may wish to take a less executive role, or some executives may retire and the board may wish to maintain their expertise. In the majority executive board, the outside directors may tend to be seen by the executive directors as there to give advice (Figure 2.2).

The Minority Non-Executive Board

To be, and be seen to be, an effective overseer or supervisor of executive management, a board needs to have a majority of independent directors. This is recognised by the corporate governance codes that must be followed by companies listed on a stock exchange. It is also adopted by other corporate entities who see an important role for the board to oversee the management. Some charities, for example, adopt this model, with only the Chief Executive, and perhaps the Finance Director, serving on the board (Figure 2.3).

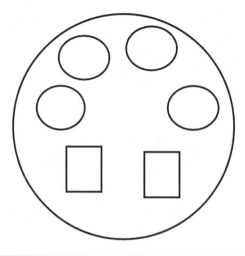

Figure 2.3 The minority executive board.

The All-Non-Executive Board

In this board model, no members of management serve on the board. In practice, the CEO and other senior executives are invited to attend board meetings to provide information and answer questions. However, they do not have a vote on board decisions, which could be taken in their absence (Figure 2.4).

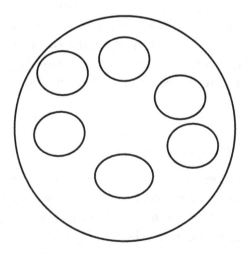

Figure 2.4 The all-non-executive board.

The Two-Tier Board

The four board models discussed thus far are known as unitary boards, because, as we will see later, they are responsible for both setting the strategy of the entity and overseeing its achievement. By contrast, in some countries, for example in Germany, a two-tier board system is used. The upper, supervisory board, consisting solely of outside directors, is responsible for overseeing the activities of the management board, which has the responsibility for setting strategy, policy and achieving results in the enterprise (Figure 2.5).

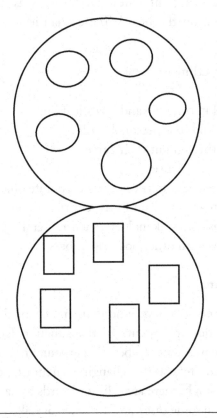

Figure 2.5   The two-tier board.

Board Size

The constitutions of some organisations regulate the size of the board, requiring a minimum, but rarely a maximum number. Calls for additional directors to represent this or that interest are frequently heard. Calls to reduce board size are seldom voiced.

Yet the number of members of a board and their balance of executive and non-executive can be critical to a board's effectiveness. Beyond eight or ten people, boards require a very skilful chair, and some directors may find it difficult to contribute fully. Such boards may also become divisive and fail to reach a consensus.

Director Qualities and Characteristics

Obviously, people bring different experiences, skills, and personal talents to their work on the board. These qualities and characteristics include:

- age, gender, ethnicity
- education
- professional knowledge and qualifications
- personality and interpersonal skills
- experience throughout their career
- board-level experience
- experience relevant to the entity's corporate objectives
- network contacts relevant to the entity's work
- relationships with stakeholders, such as members or employees
- relationships with other board members

The Balanced Board

A board clearly needs to have, among its members, those skills, experiences, and abilities appropriate to the situation facing that entity. Unfortunately, boards tend to be self-perpetuating and to grow old together, failing to reflect the changing circumstances facing their enterprise. Increasingly, there are calls for boards to have a greater gender diversity and, in some cases, a wider range of stakeholders, as we will discuss later. We will also consider succession planning or future board membership, but for now the corporate governance worksheet that follows will highlight strengths of the current situation on your board.

Corporate Governance Workbook

Worksheet #2

This worksheet focuses on material in this chapter. At this stage, do not be concerned about board processes, board leadership, or interpersonal issues within the board.

1. Describe the board structure

    Complete the board circle and management triangle diagram again, for the corporate entity whose governance you are describing. Number each member shown on the board so that you can write notes about each position (Figure 2.6).

2. Now consider each position on the diagram. Write a brief profile for each of your colleagues on the board. Cover the following:

    • age, gender, ethnicity
    • education
    • professional knowledge and qualifications
    • personality and interpersonal skills
    • experience throughout their career
    • experience particularly relevant to this entity
    • board-level experience
    • experience relevant to the entity's corporate objectives
    • network contacts relevant to the entity's work

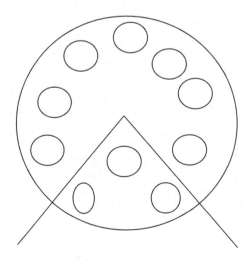

Figure 2.6   Board circle and management triangle.

- relationships with stakeholders, including members, employees, and others
- relationships with the other board members

3. What are the strengths of the board? Consider overall experience, financial knowledge, relevant expertise.
4. Are there any weaknesses of the board? Consider overall experience, financial knowledge, relevant expertise.
5. What is your opinion of the board size: too small, about right, too large?
6. Consider the balance of the current board between executive and non-executive directors (both independent and connected non-executives). In your opinion, is this balance appropriate?
7. Looking ahead, how might this be changed, and how could this be done?
8. Has any thought been given to such issues on your board?

3

THE ROLE OF THE BOARD

What Do Boards Do?

Surprisingly perhaps, boards seldom give much thought to the work they do and whether they do it effectively. The agenda of many traditional board meetings are predictable: apologies, minutes of the last meeting, matters arising, report from the chief executive, financial report, and so on to 'any other business. What should boards be doing? How should they allocate their time? The following template may help.

Strategy Formulation

The formulation of strategy involves thinking about the future that the board wants and expects for their organisation. The strategic direction set by the board establishes the long-term objectives for the organisation and creates its image. Strategy formulation is neither long-range planning nor budget forecasting. The time horizon for strategic thinking depends on the nature of the enterprise: the directors of a retail store, operating from rented premises, may look ahead no more than three or four years, whereas the board of the electricity-generating company must look ahead a decade or more, because of the long time and heavy cost of building a generating plant. Strategy formulation means identifying uncertain future events, alternative economic, political, and social scenarios, and identifying acceptable risks.

There are many approaches to strategic thinking and plenty of advisers willing to help.

Strategy formulation is a fundamental part of every board's responsibility and time needs to be spent on it, however ambiguous, challenging, and uncertain the future may look.

DOI: 10.1201/9781003321132-3   **17**

Policy-Making

Policies are set at every level in an organisation: board-level policy should stem directly from the board's strategy and guide decisions throughout the organisation. Boards need to establish policies for the entire organisation, for example, on markets and products, on finance and borrowing, on safety and security, on sustainability and the environment, and on human resource management and labour relations.

Executive Supervision

The third basic function of every board is overseeing management performance, in the short and longer term. The board needs to ensure that the expected performance is being achieved, that board policies are being followed, and that relevant issues are being reported by management.

Accountability

Boards are responsible to their members, whether they are the shareholders of a company, the members of a professional organisation, or the partners in a partnership. Reporting requirements, such as annual accounts, will probably be covered in the entity's constitution. In many cases, of course, the law applying to companies, partnerships, and other regulated entities, lays down the minimum requirement for financial reporting and often calls for further reports, for example, on corporate strategy, employee relations, and environmental concerns.

In today's culture of instantly available information, the members may, increasingly, expect wider access to information about the enterprise; while the development of social media and Internet access to organisations' information provide bountiful opportunities, together with some challenges, as we will discuss in a later chapter.

Performance and Conformance Roles

Further study of Figure 3.1, the quadrant of board activities, shows that the right-hand board activities – strategy formulation and policy-making – concern the direction of the organisation, its goals,

Accountability	Strategy formulation
Executive supervision	Policy making

The past   The present   The future

Figure 3.1   The quadrant of board activities.

objectives, and direction. In other words, they are about performance: they are about the future (Figure 3.2).

By contrast, the activities on the left of the quadrant – executive supervision and accountability – concern the achievement of budgets and plans, compliance with regulation and reporting expectations. In other words, they are about conformance: about the present and the past.

There is a natural harmony across the four aspects of the board activities – the formulation of strategy leads to the making of policies and plans; the performance of the executive management against those policy and plans is then supervised by the board, which leads to reporting their accountability to the members and, where appropriate, other stakeholders and society. It should be a continuous cycle.

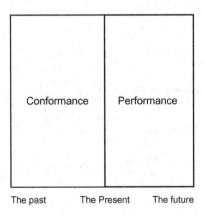

Conformance	Performance

The past   The Present   The future

Figure 3.2   The board's performance and conformance roles.

Allocating the Board's Time

If you ask directors how boards *should* allocate their time, between the four board activities, you will usually be told 'about equally, perhaps an emphasis on strategy formulation.' However, if you ask them to reflect on how their boards *actually* spend their time, you get a different answer. Having run this exercise with hundreds of directors, the result is remarkably consistent. Although directors, almost unanimously, agree that they should be allocating a significant part of their time to strategy, the reality, they explain, is that strategic considerations get overshadowed by executive supervision issues that need immediate attention. To respond to this dilemma, some boards dedicate an occasional board meeting, or even two or three days, to strategy formulation.

Board and Management Relations

Governance is not management, as we have already seen. So, boards must work through their management. In boards dominated by executive directors, this may not be so difficult, although it might then be argued that, as far as executive supervision is concerned, the board is 'marking its own examination paper.' In boards dominated by outside, non-executive directors, particularly in the all-non-executive board, the relationship between the board and its management is crucial.

All boards need to work through their management. Figure 3.3 endeavours to demonstrate this linkage with a central activity at the heart of the board activity matrix.

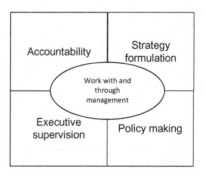

Figure 3.3   The link between the board and management.

The significance (and thus the size) of this central linkage can vary considerably. At one extreme, a board might determine the corporate strategy, establish board policies, oversee the executives, and maintain accountability on its own, making the decisions, giving instructions, and leaving management to carry them out. At the other extreme, a board might delegate much of the responsibility for strategy formulation and policy-making to their Chief Executive and executive management. This is the case in many large, listed companies. Nevertheless, the board still has overall responsibility for the direction of the enterprise and directors need to be fully aware of the strategic situation and approve strategic objectives, plans, and policies. Boards cannot delegate their entire responsibility for strategy formulation and policy-making to their management, as occurs in two-tier boards.

In boards consisting entirely of outside, non-executive directors, it is usual for the board chair to invite the CEO and, possibly, other senior executives to attend board meetings to provide information, answer questions, and give advice. However, in such cases, these executives do not have voting rights, and board decisions can, of course, be made in their absence.

In two-tier boards, responsibility for strategy, policy, and the executive management of the enterprise are the responsibility of the management board. The supervisory board's role is to question and understand strategies and policies, signing-off on them or referring them back to management for further action.

The work that the board does is fundamental to effective corporate governance. Attention to the role of the board in practice should be a primary concern of all board members.

Corporate Governance Workbook

Worksheet #3

This worksheet relates the material in this chapter to the work of your board.

1. Use the template of Figure 3.4 to answer the following questions:
   a) In an ideal world, for a board like your own, how should the directors spend their time in board meetings? Show the percentages in each of the boxes in the quadrant.

Accountability	Strategy formulation
Ideal % Actual %	Ideal % Actual %
Executive supervision	Policy making
Ideal % Actual %	Ideal % Actual %

Figure 3.4 How my board should allocate its time ideally, and how it actually does.

b) How does your board *actually* spend its time in board meetings? Think back on the agenda of recent meetings, were you formulating strategy, making policy, overseeing the work of management sorting out ongoing problems, or being accountable to members and other stakeholders?

2. Reflecting on your answers to question 1, are you satisfied with this situation, do things need to change, if so, how might that be achieved?

3. How does your board go about formulating strategy?

4. What is the strategic time horizon that is appropriate to the activities of your enterprise? Do your board colleagues think at this distance?

5. What are the goals, objectives of your entity? What is your vision of its long-term future? Is this vision shared by your board colleagues?

6. Are you satisfied with the board-level policies created by the board? How might they be improved?

7. In fulfilling the board's responsibility for supervising executive management, are you satisfied with the existing situation? Is reporting adequate? How might it be improved?

8. Does your board fulfil the requirement to be accountable to members and other stakeholders adequately? If not, how might it be improved? Consider, not only regular, routine written reports, but other ways of interacting with them.

9. How does your board work with and through management? How might this be improved?

10. Building on your answers to questions 3 and 4 in the previous work-sheet #2, and thinking overall about the way your board works, what are its strengths and weaknesses? What are the opportunities for improvement?

4

THE CORPORATE ENTITY AND SOCIETY

The Scope of Corporate Governance

We are now able to review the scope of corporate governance, to consider who is directly involved and to recognise who can be affected by corporate governance decisions. Those involved in the governance of corporate entities are shown in Figure 4.1.

Corporate entities are incorporated to meet the needs of their members. In the case of limited-liability companies that is the group of shareholders with voting rights defined by the articles of association, in the case of clubs, cooperatives, professional bodies, and trade unions it is the fully paid up members, with rights under the entity's constitution, in the case of partnerships, the members are the partners, with rights given by the partnership agreement they have signed. Their boards are central to their governance. Members appoint their directors in line with the constitution – executive directors, connected non-executive directors, and independent non-executive directors.

The board is the linchpin between the members and the management of the enterprise. But, as Figure 4.1 shows, this central governance structure must interact with a range of other interested parties. These include *the contractual stakeholders*, those with a direct contractual link with the entity, such as the employees, the suppliers of goods and services, including all the firms in the supply chain, and firms in the ultimate delivery chain, up to the ultimate customers or consumers.

The financial stakeholders include financial institutions and other sources of non-equity (that is non-shareholder) funding. For quoted companies, financial intermediaries are often involved. The creditors also have an interest because they are providing part of the entity's working capital.

DOI: 10.1201/9781003321132-4

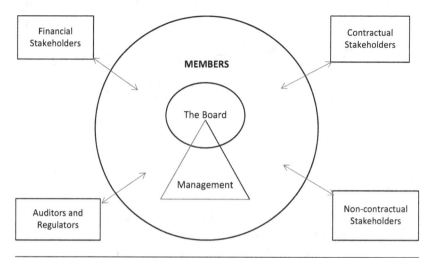

Figure 4.1   The scope of corporate governance.

Non-contractual stakeholders who are interested in the governance of the entity include competitors, the media and interest groups. Local, national, and international communities and governments, wherever the entity operates, may also have interests. Increasingly, the entity's effect on the environment, climate change, and sustainability needs to be considered.

Auditors and regulators are another interest group in the corporate governance field. Entities appoint independent, outside auditors in line with their constitution. Nation state, provinces, and cities also affect corporate governance through relevant laws, ordinances, and regulations. Stock exchanges also require listed companies to follow their listing rules. Consider the implications of Figure 4.1 in more detail.

Contractual Stakeholders

Employees

Employees are the most significant resource in any corporate entity. All boards have a vital responsibility to the employees in their organisation, whatever the form of that corporate body. It is the duty of the board to ensure that corporate policies exist, either as board policies or policies designed by management to ensure that conditions of employment are pursued consistent with the organisation's culture, as well as meeting the demands of labour law. The board should not only insist that such policies exist but that systems are in place to ensure they are followed continuously and updated when necessary. If other firms are involved in a supply chain, particularly if any are overseas, the board may want to ensure that they also have appropriate employee policies: failures could reflect on them.

Suppliers of Goods and Services

Most purchasing decisions are made by management. But boards have a basic corporate governance responsibility to ensure that board policies are created, or management policies approved, that cover all buying decisions, including price negotiation, tendering practices, ensuring suppliers meet employment, safety, and environmental norms and the identification and control of vested interests. Decisions on strategically significant contracts may be reserved for the board. Systems are also needed to ensure that these policies are followed.

Firms in the Supply Chain

In considering relations with suppliers, boards need to consider their entire supply chain. Failure of a firm in the supply chain to follow the board's own policies could result in reputational and financial loss. Consequently, board policies need to apply along supply chains with systems to ensure compliance.

Firms in the Delivery Chain

Similar considerations apply to organisations in the down-stream delivery chain, for example firms supplying distribution or transport services, warehousing, wholesale and retail sales. Policies need to meet the board's approach to business, with systems to ensure compliance.

Customers and Consumers

The long-term success of every enterprise hinges on the consistent satisfaction of its customers and users of its products or services. Boards need policies that monitor customer satisfaction, supported by accurate, relevant, and up-to-date information. Directors need to know, not only the latest revenue figures, but how their customers see them.

Financial Stakeholders

In addition to the contractual stakeholders directly involved with the entity's activities, boards also need to be aware of their financial stakeholders, who are relevant to their corporate governance. Consider some of them:

Lenders and Other Sources of Non-Equity Funds

The source of its funding is crucial to every enterprise. The balance between equity funding, provided by shareholders capital, and external borrowing (often called the gearing or leverage) can be critical, because it reflects the exposure of the entity to financial risk. Directors need to be aware of sources of funding, regularly updated about these sources and the terms of borrowing, including interest rates, repayment terms, and security pledged. Financial institutions and the instruments on which borrowing is arranged vary considerably but, in every case, the financial institution has an interest in their clients' governance.

Stock Markets and Financial Institutions

For a company whose shares are listed on a stock exchange, that stockmarket, the stockbrokers, financial institutions, and other intermediaries involved, are fundamental to the company's governance. Boards need to be sensitive to their relations with the market and its members, constantly working to maintain and improve the standing of the company's reputation, reflected in its share price. We will discuss links with the shareholder members and investor relations in a later chapter.

Creditors

Suppliers and contractors provide all firms with a continuing source of working capital by extending credit. Consequently, creditors are also financial stakeholders with an interest in governance. Boards need to ensure that suitable policies exist for relations with creditors to maintain credit worthiness.

Non-Contractual Stakeholders

We come now to the set of stakeholders which does not have a contractual relationship with the entity but, nevertheless, has a very real interest in its corporate governance.

Competitors

Strategy formulation is a fundamental part of every board's responsibility, as we have seen. Competitors, both existing and potential, are a major component in every strategy. Consequently, directors need an up-to-date knowledge of their entity's competitive situation, both currently and potentially over its strategic time horizon.

Some competitors will be obvious because they are currently offering competing goods or services. However, customers' needs might be met in the future in unexpected ways, from unanticipated sources. As part of their ongoing strategy formulation, boards need regular updates on the overall competitive situation facing their operations, with imaginative insights into possible future developments.

Local Communities

Inevitably, all corporate entities affect the communities in which they operate. They can have a negative impact on their local community, for example by creating traffic congestion, noise pollution, or the threat of unemployment. Conversely, of course, entities do have a positive effect on their local communities, not only by providing goods or services and employment but, for example, by bringing trade or other activity to the district, enhancing the standing of the community, or by specific projects that enhance community life. Directors need an awareness of the possible effects, good or bad, that their enterprise might have on the local community, both in the short and the strategic long term.

National and International Communities Where the Entity Operates

Corporate entities that operate at the national or international level, obviously, have an impact far beyond the local communities in which they operate. Boards need to ensure that their corporate activities not only meet relevant laws and regulations but reflect the culture of the places involved. Directors need to be aware, for example, of possible impacts, throughout their organisation, of labour practices in foreign subsidiaries or their supply chains, or of the implications of aggressive tax planning that shifts the burden of tax from high-to low-tax countries.

An important role for outside, non-executive directors can be to raise questions about the national or international impacts of strategic decisions, as well as monitoring ongoing corporate activities for their cultural and community implications.

The Environment, Carbon Emissions, and Sustainability

Societies' concern for the environment, climate change, and sustainability is an area of growing significance for the modern board. In the past, many boards felt that they met their social obligations by fulfilling the laws and regulations where they operated. It was up to the government to set the rules. Today, society tends to expect more of corporate entities. Indeed, the call is for organisations to fulfil governance and social expectations, as well as meeting their economic objectives in what is termed ESG (environment, society, and governance). The need to move towards zero carbon emissions is crucial to society.

Auditors and Corporate Regulators

Finally, we come to the fourth set of stakeholders in the scope of corporate governance (Figure 4.1) – the outside auditors and the corporate regulators.

Independent Outside Auditors

Almost invariably, a corporate entity's constitution provides for the audit of the financial reports, presented by the directors to the members, to be audited by independent, outside auditors. Although small entities might appoint auditors from among the members, as was the case with limited companies in the 19th century.

Company law also requires the appointment of independent auditors and, in some jurisdictions, calls for audit firms to change the partner responsible for the audit regularly and for companies to change their auditors periodically, to avoid overfamiliarity between audit staff and their client.

We will discuss the work of the board audit committee and their relationship with the independent auditor later.

Corporate Regulators

Company law lays down the rules for the incorporation of limited-liability companies and the requirements for filing details of directors, company secretary, and registered office, and specifies the financial and other reports that companies must routinely deliver. Companies whose shares are listed on a stock exchange must also satisfy the exchange's listing rules.

Organisations registered under other legislation, such as charities, cooperatives, and credit unions need to follow the relevant law and meet the reporting requirements of the appropriate regulator. Other legislation, for example concerning health and safety, environmental protection, or the application of political sanctions, may also apply to any corporate entity.

We have now briefly discussed the relationships of boards and their directors with their various stakeholders, including the contractual stakeholders, such as employees and firms in the supply and delivery chains; the financial stakeholders, which provide funding for the entity; the non-contractual stakeholders, including local, national, and international communities; and the independent auditors and corporate regulators.

In Chapter 5 we will look at the workings of the board and the role of the Chair. Before that, the following worksheet relates the material in this chapter to the work of your own board.

Corporate Governance Workbook

Worksheet #4

Refer to Figure 4.1. You have already considered the members of your corporate entity and reviewed your colleagues on the board in the previous three worksheets.

In this worksheet you will consider the four groups of stakeholders, involved in your corporate governance. Given the diversity of organisations, please use the questions as a prompt to building your own perspective on your corporate situation.

Turning first to the *contractual stakeholders*:

1. Considering your employees: List the numbers in categories, such as senior staff, middle management, and employees in all branches, divisions, or subsidiaries, including part-time and casual workers, and people on contracts who might be considered employees. Does the organisation have retired workers to whom they still have a commitment?

2. Are you satisfied that the board has regular and sufficient information about its employees? If not, what needs to be done? As a director, how do you judge the morale of your employees? Are they satisfied with the organisation? Should the board be taking any action in connection with the employees?

3. Identify and categorise the next set of contractual stakeholders – the *suppliers of your goods and services*. Review the board policies on suppliers. Do they provide adequate control of choice and terms, pricing and tendering, and the control of possible conflicts of interest?

4. If your goods or services are supplied through a *supply and delivery chain*, identify those contractual stakeholders, including remote suppliers, shippers, warehousing, transport contractors, distributors, and retailers. Are the board policies adequate to ensure that they abide by your corporate policies?

5. Identify the *customers or consumers* of your organisation's output or services. How does the board monitor the ongoing satisfaction of these contractual stakeholders? Is this adequate; if not, what needs to be done?

Turning now to the *financial stakeholders*:

6. Identify any financial institutions, organisations, or individuals to whom your organisation has a financial commitment. Identify and categorise these, noting the sums involved, and terms including interest rates, repayment terms, and security

required. How heavily geared is your enterprise? Is this level of financial risk appropriate?

7. Is the board sufficiently aware of the significance of creditors as a source of working capital? Are the board policies in this area adequate? Are they being followed?

Now focusing on the *non-contractual stakeholders*:

8. As a director, are you confident of your knowledge about *competitors*, both actual and potential? Are there ways in which the goods or services offered by your entity could be met in a different way? Does your board discuss such matters?

9. What beneficial impact does your entity have, or could have, on your *local community*? What adverse impact does your entity have, or could have, on your local community?

10. Does your entity operate at the national or international levels? If so, is the board sufficiently aware of the potential cultural or community impacts of these activities? How is that information obtained? Do the outside, non-executive directors accept a responsibility for questioning the cultural and community implications of strategic decisions? Do they have sufficient information to do that effectively?

11. Does your board reflect society's growing concern for the environment, climate change, and sustainability? Does the board have regular information on ESG (the Environment, Society, and Governance)? Do you consider that your organisation meets governance and societal expectations, as well as meeting the objectives in its constitution?

Finally, focusing on *audit and regulatory matters*:

12. Who are the auditors of your corporate entity? How are they appointed? Has consideration ever been given to changing them? Have their recent audit reports been unqualified? Are the auditors genuinely independent of your organisation?

13. Is your corporate entity registered under specific legislation? If so, which act(s)? (e.g., Companies Act, Partnership Act, the law of charities, trade unions, or cooperatives, or other regulations). How does your board ensure that it is meeting all the

requirements of the law and regulations? How do the directors ensure that formal reporting requirements are being met?

14. Look again at Figure 4.1: Are there any other sets of organisations or individuals who might legitimately be considered to fall within the scope of your corporate governance? If so, how does the board relate with them?

5

BOARD CULTURE AND THE CHALLENGE OF THE CHAIR

On Board Culture

Writers on corporate governance often emphasise the importance of board-level 'culture,' but seldom explain what they mean by 'culture,' a word that cloaks a range of ideas. In essence, a culture reflects the shared beliefs, expectations, and values of a country, a community, or, indeed, a board of directors. A culture can be influenced by external economic, political, and social factors, as well as past events, traditions, language, and, above all, leadership.

The culture of a board reflects its attitudes to authority, relationships, and values. The culture determines what is considered acceptable, right or wrong. It affects how those involved behave. Board culture can accelerate or slow down change. Board cultures evolve over time, as circumstances, leaders, and members change. In other words, board culture mirrors 'the way things are done around here'; it can be nebulous and opaque, but all board cultures have attributes that can be studied.

Characteristics of Board Culture

Board culture can be influenced in many ways. Here, we consider a few of the more significant. First and foremost is board leadership: a new board chair can change board culture overnight.

Board Leadership

Board leadership typically comes from the board chair but can be assumed by a dominant individual or by other directors if the chair is weak. Leadership styles vary. A professional leadership style encourages *all* directors to contribute to board deliberations, with people

DOI: 10.1201/9781003321132-5

respected for their experience, knowledge, and wisdom. In other boards, however, authority is jealously guarded by one or a few of the directors, with other board members expected to accept their lead, commenting only when called on.

Board Size

The size of the board also affects its style: too many members and the opportunity for individuals to contribute is limited, and the board may divide into factions; too few and there may be insufficient diversity of opinion or experience.

Board Structure

The balance of the board between independent, connected, and executive directors will clearly affect board deliberations.

Board Members – Personal Characteristics

The experience, knowledge, and skills among the directors are significant factors in determining board style.

Board Adaptability

Some boards are slow to recognize and adapt to changing circumstances. Other boards adapt readily, with flexible responses to changing situations.

Board Collaboration

Members of professional boards support each other, ensuring that everyone understands and is involved and committed. At the other extreme, board members compete, showing distrust, and even hostility towards one another.

Board Conflict

Board-level conflict can be either desirable or destructive. Conflict that is creative with tough-minded, but courteous, interactions between members, who say what they believe, but try to understand conflicting points of view, is found in successful boards. In others, conflict and political infighting can damage board relationships and harm the corporate entity.

Board Relationships

In some boards, directors see themselves as part of a board team and treat each other with frankness, respect, and trust. In others, directors act as individuals, distrusting or disliking some colleagues. In such cases, image-building, posturing, and boardroom games can occur.

Board Tradition

In some boards, rituals and customs mean a lot. Corporate stories and traditions are frequently mentioned. Board procedures and precedents are well established. Many members of such boards are likely to be long serving. There is probably a formal board room and there may be pictures of past chairs on the wall. At the other extreme are boards with no time for tradition, in which board practices evolve readily. The average length of directors' service may be relatively short. Informality is the keynote of their meetings, which are held wherever and whenever it is convenient.

Commitment

In some boards, members show a low commitment to the board and the organisation, with high levels of self-interest. At the other extreme, all directors are highly committed to the corporate entity, the board, and their fellow directors.

Communication

Access to information is a source of potential board-level power. Consequently, in some boards, directors guard the information they have, protecting their sources and encouraging secrecy. Gossip and grapevine communication prevail. Other boards, however, seem to encourage open communication, with a ready exchange of data, information, and knowledge.

Conformity

Some board chairs, believing that a board should be united, expect their directors to conform to group norms. Non-conformists are not tolerated; indeed, they are unlikely to be appointed. By contrast, other chairs welcome non-conformists, recognising that they can bring fresh insights, challenging board thinking.

Corporate Accountability

The duty of accountability is not high on the agenda of some boards, believing that the audited financial accounts and director's report will suffice. Other boards have the interests of their members and other stakeholders very much in view and supplement the minimum required disclosures with events, publications, and regularly updated websites that seek to inform and involve those in the scope of their corporate governance.

Corporate Policy-Making

Some boards are closely involved in corporate policy-making, working with management to ensure that appropriate policies exist, covering relations with customers, employees, suppliers, and all other parties involved with and affected by the organisation. Other boards, however, believe that policy-making is the role of management and pay little attention to this concern.

Corporate Supervision

Many boards spend a lot of their time overseeing operational matters and supervising their management, sometimes involved in 'fire-fighting' current problems. Micro-management from the board room will cause problems. At the other extreme, other boards delegate much to their chief executive and senior management, relying on reports and seldom getting directly involved in management matters.

Corporate Vision

This attribute indicates the extent to which directors share a strategic perspective on the company's present position, its strategic direction, and its future prospects. In some entities, the directors can readily articulate the entity's mission and strategic situation; in others, directors either do not understand the strategic context or, worse, disagree on what it should be.

Decision-Taking

Decision-taking may be strongly influenced by one person or a small group of directors, in which case there may be little analysis and many dogmatic statements. In such situations the chair may play a dominant role. Alternatively, decisions may be reached only after sound discussion, leading eventually to a consensus among all directors.

Innovation

Some boards expect all innovation to be driven by the CEO and the top management team. In others, each director is expected to contribute new ideas. In some boards, all ideas are welcomed, even if controversial. In others, past successes influence views on the future, new thinking is discouraged, developments are expected to fit established norms, change is resisted.

Status

Directors' perception of their status is important in some boards. In such cases, titles are important and meetings often formal, the boardroom may have status symbols and elaborate directors' dining. Conversely, in other boards status is relatively unimportant, directors not needing ego-reinforcing signals to be sent to the rest of the organisation or the outside world.

Trust

Corporate governance is founded on trust. Legally, this involves the fiduciary duty owed by directors to their members. But the relationship between directors also plays an important part. In some boards, directors trust each other implicitly. While in others trust is low and directors suspicious of each other's ability or motives.

Identifying the cultural characteristics of a board is a matter of personal perception. Indeed, for a given board, directors might identify other characteristics that are not embraced by those mentioned above. However, the cultural characteristics listed can be used to identify different styles of board behaviour.

Identifying Board Behaviour

Obviously, the dynamics of boardroom behaviour vary considerably. Boards differ in their culture and, therefore, have different board styles. The cultural characteristics we have just considered can be used to identify board styles. Some of the cultural characteristics reflect the way board members work together; while others reflect how the board works to achieve its objectives. The challenge is to balance concern for board relationships with concern for achieving corporate success.

The simple matrix in Figure 5.1 contrasts this concern for relationships between board members with its concern for getting the job done.

Some boards score well on both dimensions and their overall style can be considered professional. Their directors are experienced, well informed, and collaborative, sometimes holding strong views and engaging in tough-minded, but amicable, discussion. In such boards

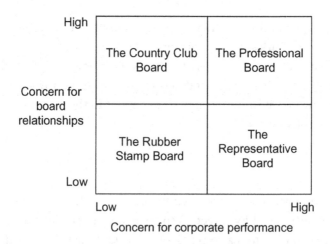

Figure 5.1   The board style matrix.

outside non-executive directors are closely involved in decision-making and share a clear view of the corporate strategy. Deliberations in such boards tend to seek consensus and votes are rarely taken. These boards, in the top right quadrant of the matrix, have a professional board style. The boards of many listed companies fall into this category.

However, the behaviour of other boards is not so professional. Over time, their board practices may have evolved into a comfortable, convivial relationship between long-standing friends. Outside directors are expected to ask questions and offer advice, but they are not expected to probe the work of the executive directors. In such entities, the climate in the boardroom is convivial, in fact, more like that of a privileged country club. Such boards are shown in the top left quadrant of Figure 5.1.

Then there is a category of entity in which the board provides little more than a legalising rubber stamp for decisions taken elsewhere. This is shown in the bottom left quadrant of Figure 5.1 In some situations, this can be appropriate, such as in the board of a subsidiary company whose directors follow orders from their parent company, or in a company incorporated to limit liability for a specific exposure, or a 'letter box' company,' formed to facilitate a tax planning scheme.

Finally, in the bottom right quadrant, boards whose members represent different interest groups are shown. For example, in the governing body of a hospital, board members might represent the medical staff, the hospital administration, the patients, and the financing institution. In such boards, members tend to take positions that reflect the interests of the groups they represent. Debates can be lively, and votes are often demanded. The governance style, in such cases, is more like that of a local authority council or a country's parliament, with opposing political perspectives.

The Role of the Chair

Chairman of the board, or the chair as the position is frequently called these days, play a vital role in every corporate entity. The constitution may define the way the chair is appointed, and the duties and powers involved. In a limited-liability company, the chair is chair of the board, not chair of the company, although that is the prestigious position often adopted.

Chairs inevitably influence the corporate governance of the enterprise. Some see the role as little more than arranging and running meetings. But the potential role for the chair is a wide-ranging leadership role. An effective board operates as a team with the chair as its leader, calling for personality, commitment, and leadership ability. The following possible duties of a board chair emphasize the importance of the role:

Leadership of the Board

This is the primary role of the chair. It influences the board's culture and style and sets the tone of board activities. The chair should play a pivotal role in determining the structure and membership of the board, interviewing new members, reviewing the performance of existing members, and should be concerned about the effectiveness of the board. To be a successful board leader, the chair needs to be a skilful communicator, sensitive to human relations, a good listener, and politically astute.

Strategic Leadership

Even if the board has delegated a lot of responsibility for developing corporate strategy to management, the directors have ultimate responsibility for the strategic direction of their enterprise. So, the chair needs to ensure that the board pays appropriate attention to strategy formulation. Every director should understand the entity's mission and strategic situation and be committed to a shared view of the strategies being followed. It is the chair's duty to ensure that this is the case.

Arbitration among Board Members

Occasionally, difficult situations arise on boards when directors strongly disagree. Personal animosity may occur as a result, affecting the harmony of the board. A competent chair will be sensitive to issues that might arise and take action to maintain board unity.

Linking the Board with Management

The relationship between the chair and the senior executive is crucial, sensitive, and often subtle. At its best, the top executive perceives the chair as a wise counsellor, someone with wide and relevant experience, and a person to be trusted implicitly, while the chair sees the top executive as the best person for the job. Occasionally the relationship can prove difficult. Typical difficulties include interference by the chair in the management of the enterprise, a clash of personalities, or dissatisfaction with management performance.

Being the Public Face of the Enterprise

In a world of instant communication and social media, the spotlight falls more often on corporate entities and their boards. Behind that interest may be concerns of members, contractual and non-contractual stakeholders in the enterprise, and investigative media and other interest groups in society. Although investor, market, and public relations activities within the organisation may meet many calls for information, situations can arise which call for the company to have a public face. This role often falls on the chair.

The Management of Meetings

Finally, we reach the more obvious responsibility of the chair – arranging and running meetings. However, to be successful, meetings need to be planned as well as run.

Planning a meeting involves arranging the agenda, agreeing the time, place (real or virtual), and deciding who should attend (in addition to board members, others might be invited to give information or advice). The chair also needs to ensure that every board member has the information and knowledge needed to understand and participate in the issue before the board.

In some entities, the agenda for board meetings is no more than a copy of the last agenda. Professional chairs ask themselves 'what issues *really* need to be considered, and have I allocated board time appropriately? The opinion of board colleagues might also be sought.

An effective chair ensures that everyone is heard, controlling the garrulous and encouraging the quiet, creating an atmosphere in which any opinion can be voiced, ensuring that discussions remain focused, and eventually leading the board to consensus and agreement.

Board Politics

Corporate governance involves a political process: the use and sometimes the abuse of power. What a director says, and sometimes more significantly what a director chooses not to say, can demonstrate their understanding of and involvement in a topic under discussion. It may illuminate their views on the subject, but in doing so reflect their personal beliefs and values, their opinions of other board members, and an awareness of others' beliefs and values.

Board members are sometimes powerful people, with high self-esteem and big egos. Some may be arrogant, self-opinionated, or even bullies. But others can be diffident, insecure, and shy. Being a good listener is a hallmark of an effective director. Sensitivity to the views of colleagues, not only hearing what they say, but deducing why they say it, creates a climate of mutual trust.

In poorly led boards, personalities and political manoeuvring can prevail; then directors will play games[1]. There may be cronyism, with deal-making alliances, coalitions, and cabals. Directors might have hidden agendas. Rival camps can appear. A director might attempt to manage the meeting, questioning the agenda, challenging the minutes, questioning procedures or the quorum, lobbying, even attempting to take over the chair. The advent of virtual meetings has amplified the potential for gameplaying to achieve one's own ends. An experienced chair will end such games immediately; with a weak chair the game player wins.

Corporate Ethics Begin with the Board

The culture of every country, company, and board relies on the ethical foundations that underpin it. The strategies and policies that boards adopt reflect different attitudes to ethics, values, and risk. One board may readily take financial risks, another may be risk averse. One board might see the employees as part of a corporate community, providing education and social facilities, even housing, while another might treat its workers as 'hands to be hired and fired.'

The board's decisions and the directors' actions set the moral compass for the entire organisation. The way the board behaves, its attitude and policies on social responsibility, interpersonal relationships, ESG (environment, society and governance), and sustainability become a template for the entity. Weak leaders create weak organisations.

Corporate values are often implicit, part of people's perceptions about expected behaviour. Decisions at every level in an entity have ethical implications – strategically in the board room, managerially throughout the organisation, and operationally in every activity. Corporate ethics are not an optional exercise in corporate citizenship; they are fundamental to the governance and management of every enterprise.

Some organisations attempt to make their values explicit through board policy statements and by publishing a code of corporate ethics. A sound ethics code emphasises corporate values and should not be a vehicle for maintaining organisational discipline. Codes of ethics reflect an organisation's value system, set standards of expected behaviour, improve ethical awareness, influence attitudes throughout an organisation; set benchmarks for self-evaluation, monitoring; and reporting, while showing stakeholders the values of the organisation.

Feedback information about adverse behaviour is vital to monitor a code of ethics. Some of this information could come from employees; although they might be deterred if they felt informing might threaten their career prospects. To reduce this problem, some boards have 'whistle-blowing' policies that aim to protect whistle-blowers, and some governments have also introduced laws to protect whistle-blowers.

We can now consider the style, the role of the chair, the corporate politics, and the ethics of your own board.

Corporate Governance Workbook

Worksheet #5

The first part of this worksheet identifies your perception of the style of your board.

1. Identify the cultural characteristics of your board, using the characteristics in the text and the scale 0–10 ('not at all' to 'fully, completely')

1.1 *Board leadership*

What is the level of board leadership in your board?

1.2 *Board size*

How appropriate is the size of your board?

1.3 *Board structure*

How do you assess the balance of executive and non-executive directors on your board?

```
0         5         10
├┼┼┼┼┼┼┼┼┼┤
```

1.4 *Board members*

Overall, how well do you assess the quality of your board members?

```
0         5         10
├┼┼┼┼┼┼┼┼┼┤
```

1.5 *Board adaptability*

How well does your board adapt to changing circumstances?

```
0         5         10
├┼┼┼┼┼┼┼┼┼┤
```

1.6 *Board collaboration*

How well does your board collaborate?

```
0         5         10
├┼┼┼┼┼┼┼┼┼┤
```

1.7 *Board conflict*

Is there conflict among the members of your board?

```
0         5         10
├┼┼┼┼┼┼┼┼┼┤
```

1.8 *Board relationships*

How do you assess the relationships between the members of your board, from poor to ideal?

```
0        5         10
|--+--+--+--+--+--+--+--+--+--|
```

1.9 *Board tradition*

Does your board have its own special traditions?

```
0        5         10
|--+--+--+--+--+--+--+--+--+--|
```

1.10 *Commitment*

How strong is the commitment of your board colleagues to the organisation?

```
0        5         10
|--+--+--+--+--+--+--+--+--+--|
```

1.11 *Communication*

How well do your board colleagues communicate with each other?

```
0        5         10
|--+--+--+--+--+--+--+--+--+--|
```

1.12 *Conformity*

How strong is the sense of conformity among your board colleagues?

```
0        5         10
|--+--+--+--+--+--+--+--+--+--|
```

1.13 *Corporate accountability*

How strong is your board sense of accountability to the members and other stakeholders?

```
0        5         10
|--+--+--+--+--+--+--+--+--+--|
```

1.14 *Corporate policy-making*

How competent is your board on its policy-making?

```
0        5         10
|--+--+--+--+--+--+--+--+--+--|
```

1.15 *Corporate supervision*

How well does your board supervise executive management?

```
0         5          10
I+++++++++I
```

1.16 *Corporate vision*

How strong is your board sense of vision of the purpose and future of the organisation?

```
0         5          10
I+++++++++I
```

1.17 *Decision-making*

How competent is your board at taking decisions?

```
0         5          10
I+++++++++I
```

1.18 *Innovation*

How innovative is your board?

```
0         5          10
I+++++++++I
```

1.19 *Status*

How concerned are your board colleagues about their status?

```
0         5          10
I+++++++++I
```

1.20 *Trust*

To what extent do your board colleagues trust each other?

```
0         5          10
I+++++++++I
```

2. We can now attempt to turn your assessment of your board's cultural characteristics into a measure of board style.

Board style assessment	A	B
Board leadership	0	
Board size		0
Board structure		0
Board members		0
Board adaptability		0
Board collaboration		0

Board conflict		0
Board relationships		0
Board tradition	0	
Commitment		0
Communication	0	
Conformity	0	
Corporate accountability	0	
Corporate policy-making	0	
Corporate supervision	0	
Corporate vision	0	
Decision-taking	0	
Innovation	0	
Status		0
Trust		0

Copy the score you have given above to each characteristic into one of the two columns below. Add any additional characteristics that you feel are unique to your board.

Column A covers those cultural attributes that contribute mainly to board relationships and B to those that contribute mainly to corporate performance. Add each column A and B and divide each answer by the number of cultural characteristics you have used in your assessment (i.e. 10, unless you have added further characteristics). The result will be two indices, which can be plotted on the board-style matrix that follows (Figure 5.2).

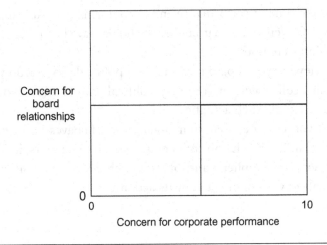

Figure 5.2 Board style matrix (blank pro forma).

You now know where you feel your board stands on the board style matrix. Obviously, the result hinges on the two variables we have used (concern for corporate performance and concern for board relationships), the cultural characteristics we have chosen, and your own personal perceptions of your board's behaviour. Consequently, the board style represented reflects your personal perspective.

Nevertheless, it will give you a marker for further development and could be used in director or board performance appraisal exercises.

3. What might be done to improve your assessment?

The second part of this worksheet is about the role of the chair, corporate politics, and business ethics.

4. Which of the possible roles of chairman, discussed in the text and listed below, does your chair adopt?
   4.1 Leadership of the board
   4.2 Strategic leadership
   4.3 Arbitration among board members
   4.4 Linking the board with management
   4.5 Being the public face of the enterprise
   4.6 The management of meetings

5. Looking back on your answers to questions 4, how do you rate your chair? Is there anything you could, or should do, to change that situation?

6. Review the agenda of recent board meetings. Was the allocation of time to performance and to conformance issues appropriate? Were there matters which should have been discussed, which were not?

7. Reviewing your board meetings as a political process, do your board colleagues (or you) play political games? How did the chair handle such activities?

8. Do you consider that your organisation behaves in an ethical manner in relation to its employees, its members, its customers, its suppliers, and other stakeholders who might be involved with or affected by its activities?

9. Does your organisation have an ethical code? If it has, does it work? If it does not, should it have one?
10. Has your board instituted a whistle-blowing policy? If it has, does it work? If it has not, should it have one?

Note

1 For detailed explanations of the games that directors play, see Tricker, Bob (fourth edition 2019) Corporate Governance – principles, policies, and practices, Oxford University Press. Chapter 14.

6

THE EFFECTIVE BOARD

The Makings of an Effective Board

The governing bodies of all corporate entities no longer expect the calm, convivial, and stress-less world of the past. All boards face decisions that need tough-minded discussion and difficult decisions. Every board can improve its effectiveness, as this chapter will explain.

The principal attribute of a board able to cope effectively with today's challenges is sound leadership supported by a well-balanced team of directors. The key characteristics of an effective board are captured by the 'six Cs' of board behaviour:

1. Commitment
   The first essential is a commitment, from every board member to the entity's mission, values, and strategy. Without a shared vision, a successful future for the organisation is unlikely.
2. Culture
   Each board develops its own culture: like people, corporate entities develop their own distinct character. Effective boards reflect the ability, integrity, and values of its members.
3. Collaboration
   Boards work as a team, each member playing a part. Effective team-play calls for communication based on trust, reliance on others, and mutual respect. Board deliberations can be challenging. Board members may need to be tough-minded, while seeking to understand other points of view. Perseverance may sometimes be needed; but so is enthusiasm, reinforced with occasional good humour, which holds the board together.
4. Competence
   A well-balanced board has the appropriate balance of experience, skills, and knowledge to make confident, reliable, and successful decisions.

DOI: 10.1201/9781003321132-6   **53**

5. Creativity

Creativity encompasses challenging conventional wisdom, exploring unconventional ideas, rather than resisting them and facilitating change. Creativity is probably the least appreciated hallmark of an effective board, yet one of the most important.

6. Contribution

An effective board needs to be achievement orientated, constantly striving to achieve the organisation's gals and satisfy members' expectations. Overall, the effective board recognises a responsibility for the long-term health and success of the entity.

Board Information

Directors have a right to the information they need to fulfil their responsibilities as directors. Obviously, different directors are likely to have different information needs. Executive directors will usually know more about the activities of the enterprise than the non-executive outside directors. Conversely, outside directors are likely to have a deeper knowledge of aspects of the worlds of finance, politics, technology, or the economic situation.

Sir Adrian Cadbury, in his UK Corporate Governance Code (1992), suggested that

> It is for chairmen to make certain that their non-executive directors receive timely, relevant information tailored to their needs, that they are properly briefed on the issues arising at board meetings, and that they make an effective contribution as board members in practice.

The same applies to executive directors, who may not be familiar with some aspects of their own organisation.

Reports and Presentations

Directors use both informal and formal sources of information. Informal sources may include conversations with colleagues, information from the media and from the Internet. From this wealth of data, they need to extract information that is relevant and reliable.

Formal sources of board information include both official reports and presentations. If it is to convey high-quality information, a report needs to be:

- *Reliable and credible*
  Readers should be able to trust the facts and rely on the conclusions.
- *Understandable*
  The level of detail, language, and content should be appropriate to potential readers.
- *Relevant*
  The content should address the issue under consideration, avoiding unnecessary detail, however interesting that may seem.
- *Comprehensive*
  All relevant aspects of the situation should be covered: half a story, like half-truths, can mislead.
- *Concise*
  Directors are often under time pressure. Verbose reports will not be given the attention they might deserve, however salient the information.
- *Timely*
  While the information in a report should be up-to-date, directors need time to read and think about the content.
- *Cost-effective*
  The collection, collation, and presentation of data are expensive. The cost of producing a report should never exceed its value in use.

Good report writing involves a skill that can be learned and improved with practice. Many board reports are produced regularly. Unfortunately, there is a tendency to produce them, even though they are no longer needed. A periodic review of routine board reports can be useful.

Presentations by senior executives, consultants, and other relevant experts can be used to provide board meetings with information and give directors an opportunity to question further.

Online Presentation of Board Reports

In the past, every month directors received the agenda for their next board meeting, supported by a pack of board papers. For many organisations, those days are over, replaced by board information delivered electronically. Software for such applications has been available for some years.[1] It is quite normal for directors to have their laptop or tablet on the boardroom table.

Accessing Information during Meetings

As well as accessing the set of formal board reports, directors may use their devices to explore other sites relevant to the topic under discussion, obtaining, for example, economic, financial, or market data, by 'googling' other websites.

In addition to the tablet or laptop, directors may also have their smart cell phones in front of them during meetings. Some chairs insist that such devices are turned off, or switched to silent, to avoid disruption. With them, directors can communicate with the outside world during the meeting, at the same time as participating in it. Directors in virtual meetings can also have access to communication devices, while they participate.

Moreover, should the need arise for more information, an executive director might say: 'I'll have my staff get that information in two or three minutes,' rather than: 'I'll have a report ready for the next board meeting.' Indeed, many now access the relevant files themselves.

Security of Board Information

Board information is valuable: in the wrong hands, both money and reputation can be lost. Since most board information is now held and transmitted electronically, the entire communication network needs to be secure. That includes the entity's own computer systems, the Internet communications, and the devices used by directors and managers.

Potential challenges with electronic communications include the following:

- failure of hardware, software, or power supply in the entity's computer systems resulting in the loss of data
- failure in Internet transmission systems resulting in loss of service and the loss of data

- unintentional errors or loss of data occurring within the information network
- unintentional distribution of information
- malicious eavesdropping for commercial espionage or fraud
- hacking to block communication, manipulation, or the destruction of data
- theft of data for fraud
- insertion of malicious content

As more corporate information is available and stored electronically, boards need to pay particular attention to cyber-security. The right of access to information must be defined and policed through access controls, which should be cyber-secure and changed frequently.

Managing Meetings, Agenda, and Minutes

Meetings need planning as well as running. In considering the agenda, the chair should answer some vital questions including the following:

What is the purpose of the meeting? The answer should not be 'to run the monthly meeting but should be based on the most important issues facing the organisation, and the vital decisions that need to be taken. Some professional chairs invite board members to suggest topics for the agenda.

- Who should attend the meeting? Obviously, its members, but consider whether others who might be invited on a non-voting basis, for all or part of the meeting, to provide information or advice. Some entities, including co-operative societies and local health and civic authorities invite members of the public to attend their board meetings, although they reserve the right, of course, to hold part of it in private (in camera).
- When should the meeting be held? The significance of items might override routine schedules.

Where should the meeting be held? Again, the regular venue may not be the best. Video-conferencing has added a new dimension to this question. Another important issue for the chair, prior to the meeting, is to ensure that all directors are properly informed and briefed on each item on the agenda. Directors cannot opt out of certain items because they lack appropriate knowledge, although they may rely on information received from fellow directors, given in good faith. Meetings of the board and its committees should be learning experiences for all involved.

Managing Virtual Meetings

In recent years, prompted by the global pandemic, many meetings of directors are held virtually. If the articles of association or governance rules do not permit virtual meetings, they should be changed.

A virtual meeting is subtly different from the conventional face-to-face counterpart. It involves different communication processes. The control of a virtual meeting is in the hands of the person who convened the meeting, sometimes called the 'facilitator' or 'host.' This may, or may not, be the formal chair of that group.

Procedures need to be established on the following points:

- who is allowed to call meetings
- the purpose of the meeting
- who should be invited to participate
- the form of the meeting – presentation, discussion on a topic, or decision-making following an agenda
- how participants indicate they want to speak
- how decisions are taken
- how a record of the meeting is kept
- who can have subsequent access to that record

Committees of the Board

Many boards form subcommittees not only to reduce the load on the main board but also to exercise control. The codes of sound corporate governance practice, enshrined by corporate governance codes and the listing rules of most stock exchanges, require companies listed on those exchanges to form three standing committees of the board:

- the audit committee
- the remuneration committee
- the nomination committee

These committees are comprised entirely (or in some jurisdictions, mainly) of outside, non-executive directors, thus making them independent of executive management. Consequently, these committees can provide independent and objective oversight, avoiding the possibility of executive domination of board deliberations.

Many private companies and other corporate entities, including not-for-profit entities, charities, NGOs, and government bodies have also adopted the concept of board standing committees to improve their own governance.

The Audit Committee

The constitutions of most corporate entities provide for the appointment of an independent, external auditor to report that the accounts show a true and fair view of the financial situation. During an audit, issues can arise that need resolving, such as concerns about financial control, or whether certain expenditure should be treated as an asset on the balance sheet or charged against that period's revenues. Such matters could be resolved between the auditor and the financial staff without the directors being aware. The audit committee acts as a bridge between the external auditor and the board. It reports to the main board, so all directors can be made aware of such matters.

Typically, the audit committee discusses the outcome of the audit, considers any contentious issues or recommendations from the auditor, receives the auditor's report, and considers the accounts before reporting to the main board. The audit committee also, usually, considers the audit fee and, if necessary, the appointment of a new auditor.

Some entities widen the responsibilities of their audit committee to include advising on corporate policies regarding risk, financial control systems, as well as environmental, societal, and sustainability reporting.

The Remuneration Committee

The remuneration (or Compensation) committee is responsible for recommending to the board the remuneration packages of executive directors, and sometimes other senior managers, including salary, bonuses and fees, pension rights, and other benefits.

The Nomination Committee

The role of the nomination committee is to recommend possible candidates for board membership. Governing bodies can, all too easily, become self-perpetuating mirrors of the existing members. Consequently, the committee needs to consider the structure of the board and its current membership to ensure that it matches the strategic future planned for the enterprise. In other words, the Nomination Committee should be concerned with succession planning, identifying potential future members and, if appropriate, developing relationships with them. In some countries, efforts have been made to increase board diversity, particularly gender diversity, and to represent a wider range of stakeholders.

Other Board Committees

Many boards create other standing board committees, such as a finance committee, an executive committee (sometimes called a 'ways and means' committee), a strategy committee, or a committee to review risk management, to reduce time pressures on the main board and to enable the subcommittee to concentrate more fully on relevant issues.

Boards might also create *ad hoc* board committees to handle specific, one-off issues. If *ad hoc* committees are created, it is important that their remit includes a clause for their eventual winding up: committees tend to exist beyond their usefulness.

Board Committee Activities

Board committees can contribute to overall board effectiveness, provided that the deliberations and decisions are carefully minuted and reported to the main board so that other directors are informed, can question, and, if necessary; become involved. The existence of board committees does not limit the responsibility of each director for the governance of the entity. If a director is unclear about or dissatisfied with a board committee matter, they must ensure that it is discussed by the entire board.

Board standing committees should be set up with a clear mandate which includes the following:

- the subcommittee's name, purpose, and duties
- the number and appointment of members
- the appointment of the committee chair
- secretarial, managerial, or professional support for the committee
- relations between the committee, management, and other stakeholders
- accountability, transparency, and reporting requirements, including circulation of committee minutes to all directors
- regular review of the committee performance and mandate

Assessing the Performance of Boards and Board Committees

The boards of many private companies and non-profit entities see no need to assess their own performance yet emphasise the importance of assessing the performance of their management with budgets, targets, and KPIs (key performance indicators). But professional governance is as important to the long-term success of a corporate entity as its management.

The boards of public, stock exchange listed companies are required by the corporate governance codes to assess board performance formally and to report that they have done so.

What would such a review of board performances involve?

What a Board Review Covers

A regular board performance assessment will:

- review the overall governance structure of the entity and the relationship with the members
- review the board structure, including the balance between independent outside directors and executive directors
- assess the balance of skills, knowledge, and experience on the board and its committees
- review the board style, efficiency, and effectiveness

- check whether directors' knowledge of the enterprise and its strategic situation is clear
- assess the effectiveness of the board's strategy formulation and policy-making
- identify director's weaknesses to be remedied by director training or by new board members
- review the policies and practices of the board and its committees
- assess the strength of management and financial controls
- review the quality, security, and timeliness of board information
- challenge director attitudes in boards with long-serving directors
- confirm the director succession plan, including the chair
- review the quality of reporting to members
- confirm that the corporate entity is compliant with all relevant law, regulations and, for listed companies, stock exchange listing rules
- provide information to respond to questions from members and other legitimate stakeholders
- review the relationship with the external auditors

A board review should take a strategic perspective, considering the directors' ability to handle long-term issues, as well as reflecting on the current situation. It is important that a review tackles 'elephants in the board room,' that is those things that everyone knows about, but no one ever mentions.

How a Board Review Is Initiated and Run

Any director can suggest a review but, typically, a board review is initiated by the chair and approved by the board. The enthusiastic support of every director is vital. Some chairs undertake the review themselves, or ask a non-executive director or their predecessor, but this inevitably lacks an independent perspective. Other boards form a special board committee, typically nominating independent directors, to undertake the review; others give the responsibility to the audit committee. Staff support may be needed if board members undertake the review.

Increasingly, however, board reviews are undertaken by outside, independent experts. This is particularly the case in listed companies, because the corporate governance codes require an externally facilitated, independent review and report, at least every three years. Consequently, board assessment advisers and specialist consultancy firms have emerged to provide board review services.

The Outcome of a Board Review

Experience has shown that board reviews often identify similar issues, including the need to spend more board time and effort on:

- corporate strategy and risk assessment
- executive succession and remuneration
- problems in the link between board and management
- domination of board discussion by management emergencies
- concern about some directors' contribution

If the board review is professionally set up, the result will not only be a report but will lead to a strategy for board and director development. That is a strategy that could bring changes in the board structure or membership, develop director competencies, rethink corporate strategies and policies, improve board information, and overall increase board-level performance. In the process, corporate governance will have been strengthened and the continuing, long-term success of the enterprise achieved.

Corporate Governance Workbook

Worksheet #6

1. *On board effectiveness*
   How effective is your board?
      Reviewing each of the six characteristics of board effectiveness in the text on a scale 0 - 10:

   1.1 *Commitment*

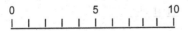

   1.2 *Culture*

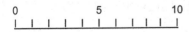

1.3 *Collaboration*

```
0               5              10
|  |  |  |  |  |  |  |  |  |  |
```

1.4 *Competence*

```
0               5              10
|  |  |  |  |  |  |  |  |  |  |
```

1.5 *Creativity*

```
0               5              10
|  |  |  |  |  |  |  |  |  |  |
```

1.6 *Contribution*

```
0               5              10
|  |  |  |  |  |  |  |  |  |  |
```

2. *On board information*

Assess the information your directors receive for board meetings against the criteria described in the text, on a scale of 0–10

2.1. *Reliable and credible*

```
0               5              10
|  |  |  |  |  |  |  |  |  |  |
```

2.2. *Understandable*

```
0               5              10
|  |  |  |  |  |  |  |  |  |  |
```

2.3. *Relevant*

```
0               5              10
|  |  |  |  |  |  |  |  |  |  |
```

2.4. *Comprehensive*

```
0               5              10
|  |  |  |  |  |  |  |  |  |  |
```

2.5. *Concise*

```
0               5              10
|  |  |  |  |  |  |  |  |  |  |
```

2.6. *Timely*

```
0               5            10
|  |  |  |  |  |  |  |  |  |  |
```

2.7. *Cost-effective*

```
0               5            10
|  |  |  |  |  |  |  |  |  |  |
```

Reviewing each of the six characteristics, what might be done to move the score closer to 10?

3. *On managing board meetings*

   Reviewing the criteria in the text, how effective are meetings in your organisation? Could anything be done to improve their effectiveness?

4. Do you hold virtual meetings? If so, how does the management of those meetings compare with the criteria described in the text?

5. *On board Committees*

   5.1 Does your board have an audit committee?

      If yes, reviewing the criteria in the text, could it be more effective?

      If no, would an audit committee be appropriate for your board?

   5.2 Does your board have a remuneration committee?

      If yes, reviewing the criteria in the text, could it be more effective?

      If no, would a remuneration committee be appropriate for your board?

   5.3 Does your board have a nomination committee?

      If yes, reviewing the criteria in the text, could it be more effective?

      If no, would a nomination committee be appropriate for your board?

   5.4 Considering any other board committees, standing or *ad hoc*, formed by your board, how might they be more effective?

6. How well do your board committees report to the main board?

7. Do your board committees have clear mandates for their activities?

    7.1 Are they effective?

    7.2 Could they be improved?

    7.3 Are they reviewed regularly?

8. Does your board have a regular board review?

    8.1 If yes, how might it be improved?

    8.2 If no, would a board review be a good idea?

9. Overall, how effective would you say your board was?

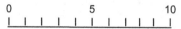

0   5   10

10. What could you do to improve that score?

Note

1 For example, see https://www.decisiontime.co.uk/board-software/, https://info.ibabs.eu/board-portal/, htps://www.boardtimeintelligence.com

7

THE EFFECTIVE DIRECTOR

To be truly effective, a director needs to understand the corporate entity being governed, contribute experience, knowledge, or other attributes to board deliberations, and be interpersonally skilful. Consider each of these three elements of effective directorship.

Understand the Corporate Entity

What does a director need to know to be *effective*? Whatever experience, knowledge, or skills a director brings to the board, whether that director is an executive director, a connected non-executive director, or an independent, non-executive director, all directors need to be familiar with the corporate entity they are governing.

A truly effective director will have:

- an appreciation of the constitution of the corporate entity, including its legal format and whether that format imposes legal responsibilities on directors
- knowledge of the members of the entity and their expectations
- an understanding of the organisation and its ongoing activities
- familiarity with the financial accounts and an appreciation of the financial situation. It is not necessary to be an accountant to make a valuable contribution as director, but every director should be broadly familiar with the income and expenditure, the financial situation, and the exposure of their enterprise to debt and risk
- sensitivity to the entity's history and culture, which can significantly affect board deliberations in long-established organisations and may need challenging
- a confident appreciation of the strategic situation of the enterprise, including its strategic context, strategic strengths and

DOI: 10.1201/9781003321132-7

weaknesses, and potential economic, environmental, political, and societal pressures likely to affect the future of the organisation.

Contribute Experience, Knowledge, and Other Skills

On many boards, the experience of directors will vary widely. Each can draw from their own experience to contribute to board thinking; although not all past experience will necessarily be relevant to the current situation.

Similarly, directors typically have different knowledge and skills, perhaps of finance and accounting, human resource management, operations and technology, marketing and distribution, the law, economics, or politics. It is vital, of course, that the knowledge is current.

Some people are invited to join a board principally for their connections, to link the organisation with important networks. Others, of course, are appointed for their reputation, title, or standing in society.

The Interpersonally Skilful Director

Just as every board develops its own unique culture, so individual directors contribute their own personality, cultural background, and interpersonal attitudes to the board. A skilful chair will be able to meld the interpersonal differences on the board into a well-functioning team. Conversely, a poor chair, lacking leadership skill, may preside over a malfunctioning, politically divisive, and fractious board.

On Joining the Board

A crucial question for the newly appointed director is:

Why have I been asked to join this board; what is expected of me? Skilful chairs will ensure that a newly appointed director has a satisfactory answer to those questions.

Executive directors, as members of management, might be presumed to have more knowledge of their organisation then non-executive directors, who will need briefing. However, even executives may not have a complete picture of the entity's operations, marketing, finances, or strategic situation. It is the responsibility of the chair to ensure that a newly appointed director is suitably briefed so that contributions are made from the outset.

Some boards use a mentoring programme, with an experienced member of the board tasked to introduce a new member into the ways of the enterprise and its board, usually quite informally. Such a relationship can help a new board member appreciate the board culture and quickly begin to contribute to board deliberations.

Some companies, particularly those with directors on the boards of group subsidiary companies, arrange induction programmes for new directors. Such programmes might include orientation on the company and the group, its activities and organisation, finances, and its strategic situation. This might be supported by visits, meetings with key personnel, and briefing sessions. Such an induction programme might also include board procedures, corporate policies, copies of board reports, and minutes of previous meetings. Without a mentor or an induction programme, a newly appointed director can only learn from experience in board meetings, which takes time.

Director Development, Training, and Updating

Professional directors realise that board membership is a continual learning process. Indeed, a few chairs ask their colleagues, at the end of a board meeting: 'what have we learned from this meeting?' Nevertheless, the rate of change in modern society makes new demands on directors. Around the world, societies' expectations of corporate entities are changing; economic, environmental, legal, and social pressures are increasing, and accountability and transparency are expected. Some societies have also become more litigious. The need for continuous director education, training, and updating is apparent; yet not all boards recognise the need.

Some directors see no reason for director-level training, believing their knowledge and experience had led to their appointment. Others recognise that in today's world, changes are occurring rapidly, knowledge is expanding fast, and past experience quickly becomes redundant.

Most corporate governance codes, which are applicable to listed companies but increasingly applied to other entities, now call for director training. Various alternative approaches exist to meet the need:

- *In-house director training programmes*
  Designed for a specific board, these programmes are typically provided by consultants or specialist firms, after a detailed analysis of board needs.
- *Board briefings*
  Led by professional experts, board briefings can provide directors with updates on changing situations in, for example, corporate reporting, economics, finance, law, the international political situation, taxation, or technology.
- *Strategy seminars*
  Again, often led by experts, strategy seminars give directors the chance to focus solely on the formulation of corporate strategy for their enterprise. Presentations may be made by management or outside experts on the strategic situation and potential uncertain future events. Discussion then follows on alternative future strategic directions and options developed and evaluated. Experience suggests that a strategy seminar should be seen as an opportunity to consider alternatives, not a decision-making board meeting. Decisions can come later at a board meeting after further analysis and review. Professional leadership and enthusiastic support are crucial.
- *Mentoring*
  Another approach adopted for the continuing development of individual directors is a one-to-one personal relationship with a trainer, who might be an external expert, a member of the management, or a fellow director.
- *Continuous self-development*
  Board experience itself can provide learning opportunities. Participating in conferences, networking with peers, and reading all provide learning opportunities. Courses in corporate governance, corporate strategy, and other board-related topics are offered by professional institutions, business schools, and specialist providers.

Today, every director faces the need to keep up to date. That means continuous learning. Successful directors know their strengths and weaknesses and try to remedy gaps in their knowledge and competence.

Director Information

Together with their board colleagues, every director is responsible for the governance of their corporate entity. That means knowing enough about its background and history, ongoing activities, finances, organisation, personnel, and the world in which it operates to make meaningful contributions to board discussion and decisions.

Directors have a right to all the information they feel necessary to fulfil their duties, and they have a responsibility to ensure they receive it. No one should say to a director: 'you don't really need to know about that!' A director needs information until satisfied that a situation is fully understood.

Some director information comes, of course, from routine financial and other reports, supplemented by one-off reports. Other corporate information may come from management presentations, Visits to corporate facilities or social gatherings, and discussions with management. But directors also obtain their information from the media, competitor communications, and other external sources, which need to be appraised critically.

Directors' Liabilities and Indemnity

In a limited-liability company, the shareholder members are not liable for the debts of the company: such limitation of liability does not extend to directors of the company. However, the legal position of directors, in most types of corporate entity, is not particularly onerous. Members expect boards to take reasonable risks to meet the entity's objectives, in line with its constitution, provided the board has acted reasonably and in the members' interest.

Of course, directors are subject to the legal sanctions of the jurisdiction in which they operate, including the law on matters such as fraud, theft, or libel. Further, boards must follow the legal requirements of any act under which their entity is registered (e.g., the Companies Act), some of which may place legal sanctions on directors for corporate wrongdoing. Directors may rely on information they receive from other directors and from board committees, unless they have grounds for doubt; in which case, they should pursue the matter, until they are satisfied.

Some corporate entities try to provide their directors with a degree of protection through director and officer liability insurance (usually known as D & O insurance). The need for such cover typically occurs where there seems to be a possibility of legal action by dissatisfied members, regulators, or others.

If in any doubt about a legal situation, a director should raise the matter with the chair or the board. If a board is then uncertain about a legal issue, it should take legal advice and, if necessary, seek the approval of the members of that entity.

Assessing Directors' Performance

A regular review of each director's individual performance is now a requirement of corporate governance codes for directors of stock exchange listed companies. This is in addition to the assessment of overall board performance, described in Chapter 6. Some corporate governance codes require the chair to hold regular development meetings with each director. The heavy demands and high expectations placed on directors of other corporate entities, not only listed companies, suggest that an assessment of individual director's performance would be valuable for most corporate entities.

Who Undertakes the Assessment?

Currently, many director appraisals are informal, conducted by the chair, discussing the outcome privately with the director involved. But there are calls for director appraisals to be more formalised. This should be approached with caution because directors often have considerable experience, strong personalities, and high self-esteem. So, a board policy, approved by all directors, is vital.

But who assesses the chair, is a legitimate question. Some chairs invite comments from their board colleagues: others prefer to have such an assessment done independently and perhaps privately. Many professional firms now offer director appraisal services: their credentials and experience need scrutiny.

What Criteria Are Used for the Assessment?

Inevitably, directors make different contributions to board discussions and decisions, depending on their experience, expertise, and personality. Moreover, these contributions can change as the circumstances facing the organisation change. So, it is important that each director knows the criteria on which the assessment is based.

Obviously, the contribution that is expected of each director needs to be known to provide the basis for the assessment. Ideally, when a director joins the board, the chair explains why the director had been chosen, including any specific expertise, knowledge, experience, or contacts that the director is expected to bring to the board; together with a briefing on the board level skills required and the time commitment expected. Such a briefing could form part of a director's orientation and induction programme.

Changing strategic circumstances facing the organisation can call for new experience, skills, or knowledge on the board. A director's attributes and core competencies, discussed earlier, can provide the pro forma for individual appraisals. Critical success factors and the risk profile of an entity may also change over time and the demands on its directors may then need to be reassessed. A regular review enables the chair to ensure that every director maintains an enthusiastic commitment to the board and the goals of the organisation.

How Is the Director Assessment Used?

An assessment of each director provides the chair with an opportunity to reinforce the chair's essential leadership role, using the opportunity to give feedback on the director's contribution to the board, both its strengths and weaknesses. The need may become apparent for further training, briefings, or visits to enhance that director's contribution. It might also highlight the need for some changes at board level. More positively, a regular, professional director assessment reinforces the achievement and commitment of the effective director.

Corporate Governance Workbook

Worksheet #7

Consider, first, how you add experience, knowledge, or skills to your own board.

1. Review each of the elements mentioned in the text and evaluate yourself, using the scale.

    Your knowledge of the constitution of the corporate entity, including its legal format and whether that format imposes legal responsibilities on its directors:

    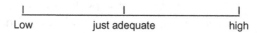

    | Low | just adequate | high |

    Knowledge of the members of the entity and their expectations. An understanding of the organisation and its ongoing operational activities:

    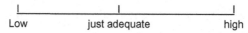

    | Low | just adequate | high |

    Familiarity with the financial accounts and an appreciation of the financial situation:

    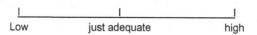

    | Low | just adequate | high |

    Sensitivity to the entity's history and culture

    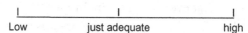

    | Low | just adequate | high |

    A confident appreciation of the strategic situation of the enterprise, including its strategic context, strategic strengths and weaknesses, and potential economic, environmental, political, sustainability issues that might affect the future of the organisation.

    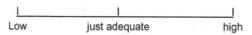

    | Low | just adequate | high |

2. What experience, knowledge, or other attributes do you contribute to board deliberations? List them.
3. Could these be enhanced? If so, how?

4. Review your interpersonal skills as a director. Do you communicate fully with the chair and all your board colleagues? Are you able to introduce new ideas, influence board thinking, and achieve results? How might these skills be improved?

5. What, if any, induction do newly appointed directors receive? Is this adequate? How might this be improved?

6. How does my board meet the need for director development, training, and updating? What could be done to improve the situation?

7. Do I have the skills and knowledge to contribute fully and responsibly to board-level activities? Is there any action I should take?

8. Does my board have director and officer insurance? If so, is it adequate? If no, should this be considered?

9. Can I access all the information I need to make a viable contribution to board discussion and decision? If not, what should be done?

10. Are there areas in which board information could be improved? If 'yes," What should I do?

11. Does your board have an individual director appraisal policy? If so, could it be improved? If not, might such a policy be worth considering?

12. Overall, am I an effective director of the board on which I serve?
What might I do to increase my effectiveness?

8

GOVERNANCE ISSUES IN DIFFERENT TYPES OF CORPORATE ENTITIES

The basic principles of corporate governance apply to every corporate entity. Nevertheless, the type and context of organisations add extra dimensions to their governance. We will consider some of these in this final chapter.

Corporate entities are defined by their constitution, which creates the locus of corporate governance power and provides the basis of corporate governance activities and structures. Corporate entities are also constrained by the laws of the jurisdiction in which they are incorporated and operate. Consequently, this chapter classifies corporate entities by the legal underpinning of their constitution and, thus, of their corporate governance.

Incorporation by Charter

- *Chartered companies*
  In Europe in the Middle Ages trading companies were chartered by monarchs or governments, for example the British East India Company, the Dutch East Indies Company, and the Hudson Bay Company. The charters created the entity and determined its governance. These companies predated the 19th century creation of the joint-stock limited liability company.
- *Chartered institutions and societies*
  Some significant corporate entities have been incorporated under a Charter from the monarch or the state. In the UK, some professional bodies, such as the Institute of Chartered Accountants, the Royal College of surgeons, and some Oxford

DOI: 10.1201/9781003321132-8   **77**

colleges, were created by their Royal Charter. These institutions or societies are, typically, founded for the benefit of their members. Their charter provides a rationale for the entity and is likely to stipulate some basic governance requirements, including the entity's name and purpose, the appointment of the governing body, and some underlying financial and governance requirements. In some cases, members of the governing body may be nominated and elected by the members of the organisation. In other cases, the members of a particular group form the governing body, for example, all full-time academic members of a college. Some charters provide a mechanism for resolving disputes through the appointment of an eminent person, perhaps known as the 'visitor.'

Around the world, universities have evolved their own form of governance equivalent to a two-tier board, combining organisational oversight with academic freedom. Although the names vary, the duality is created by a Council, with independent members representing interests in the University and community, and a Senate, with all or representatives of the academic staff. The Council oversees the University as a whole, ensuring that it continues to meet its objectives, appoints the Vice Chancellor, and ensures that the facilities and finances of the institution are sound. The Senate is responsible for the running of the University and its activities, facilities, and services, setting policies and maintaining academic standards. Some businesspeople find University governance unwieldy and complicated: their more 'business-like' approach, however, finds little favour with academics, who see the need for representation, transparency, the preservation of academic freedom, and university traditions.

Incorporation under Sector Legislation

- *Cooperative societies*
- *Savings and loan associations/building societies*
- *Trade unions*

Economic and social changes during the 19th century fostered the development of new 'self-help' entities created for the benefit of their members. These included savings and loan associations/building societies, retail cooperative societies, and credit unions. Although some have disappeared, many continue to flourish in a modern form.

Over the years, laws were enacted to regulate the behaviour of such entities. Consequently, those responsible for their governance must meet both the requirements of their own constitution, and the law relating to their business sector.

Retail cooperative stores are well known, some with supporting wholesale cooperative societies. The cooperative movement has also been adopted for the benefit of farmers, manufacturers, and other sectors around the world, offering the benefits of shared purchasing or marketing services. Cooperative societies are, typically, owned by their members, who invest in the entity, sometimes only a nominal sum, with dividends based on usage being added to their accounts. Members have the right to nominate and elect members of the governing body, which reports to those members. In many countries, cooperative societies are regulated under cooperative and community-benefit legislation, which includes the registration and reporting of societies and covers insolvency and the disqualification of directors.

US savings and loan associations and UK building societies provide mortgage-based housing loans using funds from savers' accounts. In both countries state regulations provide governance controls in addition to the entities' own constitutions.

US labour unions and UK trade unions are associations of workers, registered under the law, to function as the legal representative of their members and the bargaining agent with employers. Members join the local branch of their union, which will typically operate under a set of rules and codes of practice, covering issues such as union membership, members' subscriptions, taking industrial action, picketing, black-listing employers, and the use of union funds for political purposes. Local branches report to their union's central office, which is governed by a national executive council, made up of ordinary members, elected at the branch level. The executive council is responsible to the membership, producing an annual report and audited financial accounts, for approval at the annual national delegate conference. In the UK, each union is itself affiliated to the national Trades Union Congress.

Trusts

- *Many education, arts, heritage, medical, and sports entities*
- *Also, many charitable trusts and social enterprises*

Corporate entities may be incorporated as trusts, with the members of the governing body being trustees for the interests of their members. In such cases, the laws covering trusteeship in the relevant jurisdiction apply. Trust law calls on trustees to act with integrity and 'in the 'utmost good faith' towards the trust, its objectives, and its members.

One of the largest corporate entities in the UK is the National Health Service (NHS), which is responsible for all the hospitals, general practitioners, dentists, and support services in the country, with 1.7 million employees. It has developed a sophisticated corporate governance system, which continues to evolve. Foundation Trusts were created in 2004, as part of the UK Government's commitment to decentralisation in the provision of health care. Each Foundation Trust provides all NHS health services, from primary care to hospitals and other medical facilities in that area. The members of the Board of Governors of each Foundation Trust are local people. This board works with a Board of Directors responsible for the day-to-day running of Trust activities. Foundation Trusts are overseen by a central agrncy.

In most jurisdictions, organisations that raise funds to provide charitable services can or must register. In the UK, the regulator is the Charity Commission. The constitution of a charity should define its purpose as solely charitable and for the public good. Such organisations then come under the charity law of the relevant jurisdiction, which typically, calls for registration, reporting, and regulation.

Charitable organisations can be incorporated in various constitutional formats: smaller charities may be unincorporated societies; others incorporate as not-for-profit limited-liability companies, while some may be chartered institutions.

The UK has a charity governance code that discusses the trustee status of members of a charity's governing body. The code includes sections on leadership, integrity, decision-making, risk and control, board effectiveness, board diversity, and the need for openness and accountability. The code is designed to help charities' governing bodies develop high standards of governance. It offers advice on good practice but is not a legal requirement (www.charityexcellence.co.uk).

Many education, arts, heritage, medical, and sports entities are incorporated as trusts. Their governors may be chosen from the relevant community. For example, a school's governing body might draw members from the academic world, past scholars, distinguished citizens, and from the local community. The school's head and representatives of the academic staff may also be members or may be invited to attend governing body meetings.

Academic institutions that are funded by the tax-payer at the local or national level (often referred to as 'the public sector') may have their governance and management policies determined by local or national government. In recent years, a move towards decentralisation of responsibilities has led to local-level governing bodies, whose constitution, purpose, and duties are determined by statute.

Partnerships

Partnerships, as a form of corporate governance, have a history long before the invention of the limited liability company in the mid-19th-century. Every jurisdiction has its partnership law: in the UK this is the Partnership Act, 1890. The foundation of governance for a partnership is the partnership agreement, in which the active partners agree on their contribution to the partnership, how the partnership is to be run, and how profits or losses are to be shared. All active partners are responsible for partnership debts, which is why many partnerships subsequently sought the protection of limited liability, by becoming a company, or from a limited liability partnership, when that format became legally available in the UK by the Limited Liability Partnership Act, 2000.

Limited Liability Companies

As we have already seen, the limited-liability joint-stock company allows shareholders to invest, without becoming liable for corporate debts: All they risk is their equity investment. Although the limited-liability company was invented to attract funds from the public, today the initial concept has blossomed into many different formats.

Public Companies

Public companies are those that through their constitution are allowed to invite the public to subscribe for their shares. Many, though not all, public companies are listed on a stock exchange, some on a number of exchanges around the world, so that their shares are bought and sold on the open market. Company law in all jurisdictions regulates the governance of public companies in considerable detail. In the United States, where companies are incorporated in a state, federal oversight is exercised by the Securities and Exchange Commission (SEC). In other jurisdictions, companies are incorporated at the country level and regulated by that country's company law. In the UK, British Commonwealth, and many other countries, corporate governance rules are laid down by that country's company law, although many practices are guided by voluntary corporate governance codes, which public companies must follow or explain why they have not. These codes are now incorporated into most stock exchange listing rules.

Shares in public companies may be held by a variety of different shareholders: institutional shareholders, such as pension funds, investment trusts, or financial institutions, as well as individuals, known as 'the retail market.'

Private Companies

The limited-liability company format has been used by huge numbers of enterprises to give their owners the protection of limited liability, not to raise funds from the public. Company laws typically make fewer demands for disclosure and reporting than for public companies. Some countries now have voluntary corporate governance codes for private companies as well as public companies.

Family Companies

Many private companies are owned by the members of a family. Family firms adopt the private company format on start-up or soon after they have become successful. The founder of a family company often starts as both chief executive and chair of the board. Subsequently, if the business survives (and many do not) these roles are split. In Chinese and Indian family businesses, the head of a family often wields power over the family company, not by company law, but because of traditional norms.

A particular challenge for family companies can arise when the shareholding passes into the second generation. If one branch of the family remains running the company, while another becomes solely shareholders, tensions can arise. The remote shareholders want dividends, while the management directors want re-investment of profits, high remuneration, and executive perks. The solution is often a family forum, separate from the board of directors, set up to resolve family issues.

Start-Up Companies

The founders of a new company are often both shareholders, managers, and the initial directors. If the company thrives, it may seek additional capital through an initial public offering on a stock exchange. However, this could lead to a dilution of the original shareholders' voting power at shareholder meetings. A solution often used is the creation of dual-class shares, in which the founders' shares have more votes than the new shares. Another challenge can then arise on succession: what happens to the founders' shares with their voting privilege?

Companies in Corporate Groups

Many private companies are wholly owned subsidiaries or partly owned associate companies in a corporate group; their shares held by and their governance determined by the board of the parent holding company. Some corporate groups are large, with hundreds of subsidiaries, held at three or four levels of subsidiary.

The board of the dominant parent company must determine the form of corporate governance to be applied throughout their group, subject to company law. Some groups are governed and managed centrally, the parent company formulating group strategy and determining group-wide policies. In such cases, control is centralised, and the boards of subsidiaries are often comprised exclusively of executive directors. Other groups, particularly conglomerates and groups operating internationally, formulate group financial strategy and broad group-wide policies, but expect its subsidiaries to formulate their own strategy and create appropriate policies. In such cases, subsidiary company boards may include independent directors with industry or local knowledge.

Companies Owned by Employees

The shares in some successful companies are owned by the company's employees, rather than remote outside investors. The rationale is that employees have a sense of ownership, which provides a motivating commitment to the organisation and reflects the corporate culture.

The employment agreement will stipulate employees' rights, including entitlement to shares, which may involve length of service or be limited to senior staff. Various ways of involving employee shareholders in governance have been developed, including employee directors, employee shareholder forums, and employee shareholder participation and communication. Of course, all must be within the relevant company law and, if the company is listed, the listing rules of the stock exchange.

State-Owned Companies

Around the world, some companies are wholly owned by the state. Sometimes, this is the result of a political nationalisation policy, sometimes as a way of encouraging a business sector, sometimes through support for a failing company or industry. Unless covered by their own specific legislation, state-owned companies must meet the requirements of the relevant company law and, if listed, the stock exchange listing rules. State-owned enterprises play a significant role in China, even though a minority of shares may be listed.

Companies Limited by Guarantee

Most companies are profit-orientated, their boards' performance evaluated by long-term profit and growth in shareholder value. Although, increasingly, attention is paid to performance on environmental, societal, and governance (ES G) factors.

However, companies can be registered by guarantee, that is with guarantors, not shareholders. The guarantors commit to contribute an agreed amount should the company fail. Creditors can look to the guarantors to support a company limited by guarantee; although, in practice, the amounts guaranteed are often quite trivial.

Many companies limited by guarantee have not-profit-objectives, their performance measured by the provision of academic, charitable, or other social services. In a company limited by guarantee, power lies, not with shareholders, but with the board, which may be appointed initially by the guarantors, but then often becomes self-perpetuating.

Moving On

In this chapter we have looked, albeit briefly, at the governance of different types of corporate entities. Although the context, the purpose and the details of their governance processes differ, the fundamental need to see governance is different from management, involving strategy formulation, policy-making, executive supervision, and accountability, are common to all. Consequently, the basic concepts we have discussed, cover all corporate entities.

There are many sources of further information for readers who want to study further. The Internet has a wealth of information. Most listed companies now discuss their corporate governance on their corporate website, often under the heading 'investor relations.' Major accounting and law firms also offer commentaries on corporate governance developments on their websites.

Some professional organisations also offer guidance on corporate governance including:

The Chartered Governance Institute, London
(see www.cgi.org.uk)
The Corporate Governance Institute, USA,
(see www.thecorporategovernanceinstitute.com)
There are also Institutes of Directors in many countries. For the UK, see www.IOD.com

Of course, there are also many books that amplify the material covered in this book, for example:

Bajpai, G N (2016), *The Essential Book of Corporate Governance*, Sage, Los Angeles

Clarke, Thomas (2nd edition 2017), *International Corporate Governance – a comparative approach,* Rutledge, Abingdon England

Leblanc, Richard (editor) (2016), *The Handbook of Board Governance – comprehensive guide for public, private, and not – for – profit board members,* Wiley, New York

Monks, Robert and Nell Minnow (5th edition, 2011), *Corporate Governance,* Wiley, New York

Tricker, Bob (4th edition 2019), *Corporate Governance – principles, policies, and practices,* Oxford University Press, Oxford

The UK Corporate Governance Code (2018) Financial Reporting Council, London www.frc.org.UK

The UK charities corporate governance code: www.charityexcellence.co.uk

A concluding thought for every member of a governing body: if you are in any doubt about a corporate governance matter, seek advice. If you are unsure about legal matters consult a lawyer; if your concern is with accounting, finance, or tax, seek advice from an accountant or auditor. If the issue is a governance matter, there are now legions of experienced independent directors, consultants, and professional bodies willing and able to advise.

The responsibility of governing any corporate entity, whatever its size, purpose, or membership, is inevitably a challenge, sometimes a puzzle, but always enormously worthwhile.

Corporate Governance Workbook

Worksheet #8

1. In which of the categories, described in this chapter, does your corporate entity fall?
2. What type of constitution does your corporate entity have? (e.g. Royal Charter, partnership agreement, memorandum and articles of association, etc.)
3. Is your corporate entity covered by specific legislation? If so, what is that act, ordinance, or set of regulations? What demands does that legislation make on your board and on individual directors?

4. What are the basic governance requirements in your constitution on the following:
   4.1 the governing body membership – the nomination and election of directors, minimum number of directors
   4.2 the duties of directors
   4.3 governing body meetings: quorum, notice required
   4.4 financial records and accounts: members' rights to financial information and directors' reports
   4.5 Independent auditors: appointment, duties, and replacement
   4.6 Director remuneration and expenses
   4.7 The liability of directors
   4.8 Ensuring financial viability and winding-up procedures
5. Who are the members of your corporate entity?
   What rights do they have?
   How does the Governing Body interact with them?
   How could this be improved?

EPILOGUE

What This Book Has Been About

This book is based on a simple precept that all corporate entities need to be governed; many aspects of that governance are common to all corporate entities, so better they are governed well. This is true whether the entity is a small club, a family business, a college, a hospital, or the companies in a global conglomerate; whether its purpose is to provide services, satisfy a social need, or make a profit; whether its members are the family owners, partners, shareholders, subscribers, or a government agency; and whereever it is located. The need for sound governance applies whatever its governing body is called (the board of directors, the committee, the council, the partners' meeting, or anything else) and whatever the members of that governing body call themselves (directors, councillors, committee members, trustees, fellows, partners, or anything else). So, whether you are an executive or a non-executive director, the chair of your governing body, the company secretary, auditor, or adviser, or a manager having to deal with the governing body, this book explains what corporate governance means to you.

Corporate governance is about the way power is exercised over corporate entities and held accountable.

The Ground We Covered

We saw how every corporate entity is defined by its constitution, which determines its legal status, outlines its purpose, defines its members, and explains how its governing body is created and the rules by which it is to be run.

We distinguished executive from non-executive directors and saw how non-executive directors could be related to the entity or be independent. We considered what made for non-executive independence and emphasised that governance was different from management.

DOI: 10.1201/9781003321132-9

Five alternative board structures were described: the all-executive board, the majority executive board, the majority non-executive board, the all-non-executive board, and the two-tier board. We considered the qualities and characteristics needed in a director and recognised the importance of a balanced board, capable of meeting the challenges facing the organisation.

We saw how the fundamental tasks for every board involved formulating strategy for the entity, determining its policies, supervising its management, and being accountable to its members, stakeholders, and society. Strategy formulation and policy-making focus on the future of the enterprise: supervision of management and accountability concern the current and past situation. Corporate governance means ensuring strategies are being set and achieved, policies followed, and members' and societies' expectations met.

The focus of every board includes the members, employees, suppliers of goods, services, and finance, customers, and competitors, as well as other stakeholders affected by corporate activities. We saw how boards needed to recognise their responsibility to society, including the local, national, and international communities involved, as well as their effects on the environment and the need for sustainability.

Each board develops a unique culture and has its own style. Corporate governance involves a political process, in which the chair plays a fundamental role, leading board colleagues. Ultimately, the board determines the culture, the values, and the success of the organisation.

We also considered what makes a board effective, identifying among other things, board information and the management of meetings. Then, standing committees of the board, the audit committee, the remuneration committee, and the nomination committee were considered, together with other board committees. Increasingly, sound corporate governance practice calls for a formal and regular assessment of the performance of the board and its committees.

Then we considered what makes individual directors effective, including director appointment, training, and information. We looked at director liability and indemnity insurance. We also recognised the growing call for performance assessment of individual directors.

Crucial Messages in the Book

Six key ideas stand out:

1. Management runs the enterprise: corporate governance ensures that it is being well run and is running in the right direction.
2. Corporate governance is not management.
3. Every corporate entity needs governance and governing well. Without governance, management has no oversight, and the organisation lacks strategic direction. Corporate governance formulates strategy, both short and long term, risk averse or speculative; corporate governance ensures policies, affecting relations with members, staff, customers, suppliers, and society. Then corporate governance supervises management and is accountable to the members, other stakeholders, and society.
4. Every board can be more effective.
   There is no governing body that cannot improve its own performance.
5. Board leadership is fundamental, creating board culture and corporate values. The challenge, the opportunity, and the responsibility of the chair is to lead, achieving corporate success.
6. Corporate governance is founded on trust.

Members trust the directors they have appointed, to show competence, foresight, and integrity in all board activities.

The contribution made by every director can be improved.

Every member of every governing body can be more effective than they are currently.

The Frontiers of Corporate Governance

Society's expectations of the organisations in their midst are increasing. Facing economic, environmental, political, and social change, pressures on boards have increased. Technology offers new challenges, not least in board processes themselves. Society demands more participation, transparency, and accountability from organisations, which presents a real challenge to all governing bodies.

A Final Word

The board's duty is to set their organisation's strategic direction, creating its corporate culture and its values. Whatever the organisation, effective corporate governance improves corporate performance and ensures long-term success for the benefit of members, all stakeholders, and society. Corporate governance is the responsibility of every board and every director – including you.

Bob Tricker
Devon, England, 2022

Index

Printed in the United States
by Baker & Taylor Publisher Services